C0-DWL-609

————The————
ILLUSIONS
————*of*————
Conventional Economics

Other Books by William H. Miernyk

The Economic State of New England (co-author)

Inter-Industry Labor Mobility

Trade Unions in the Age of Affluence

The Economics of Labor and Collective Bargaining

The Elements of Input-Output Analysis

Impact of the Space Program on a Local Economy (with others)

Simulating Regional Economic Development (with others)

Economics

Air Pollution Abatement and Regional Economic Development (co-author)

Regional Impacts of Rising Energy Prices (co-author)

Regional Analysis and Regional Policy

—The—
ILLUSIONS
of
Conventional Economics

■

By William H. Miernyk

West Virginia University Press
Morgantown 1982

Copyright © 1982 by William H. Miernyk
All rights reserved

First Printing, 1982

Printed in the United States of America

ISBN Number 0-937058-14-9

812—4340

HB
71
M625
1982

For Briana,

whose generation, I hope, will have
replaced today's illusions with the
knowledge required to face the future
realistically and courageously.

Table of Contents

INTRODUCTION AND ACKNOWLEDGMENTS

The issues discussed in this book are based on the ideas of two great economists whose views fall outside the purview of "conventional" economics. They are Nicholas Georgescu-Roegen, who has developed a new paradigm called *bioeconomics*, and Wassily Leontief, the inventor of input-output analysis. It will be obvious to anyone familiar with their work that my intellectual debt to them is enormous.

Except for parts of the introductory and concluding chapters, the issues discussed here first appeared in the weekly column I write for *The Charleston Gazette*. There has been much rewriting, but parts of a number of columns have been transferred to this volume verbatim. I want to thank *The Gazette's* publisher, Ned Chilton, for encouraging me to write the column, and the many readers who have taken time to write to me about it.

I am grateful to Carla Uphold, my secretary, who typed drafts as the manuscript went through a number of metamorphoses. I also want to thank Dee Knifong, who not only corrected galleys, but handled many other details in getting the manuscript ready for the printer. And I want to thank Dr. Virginia Klenk, of the West Virginia University Department of Philosophy, who read an earlier draft with meticulous care. Her advice and criticism greatly improved the manuscript. Since I did not accept all her suggestions, at least without modification, neither she nor anyone elso who helped with this project should be held accountable for the final result.

Finally, the ideas of a number of contemporary authors are subjected to criticism in this volume. The tone is often polemical. But the criticism is never intended to be *ad hominem*. Ideas, not individuals, are the issue.

W.H.M.

Chapter 1

MYTHS AND ILLUSIONS

The Illusion of an Economic Transition

Modern economics is in a state of disarray. The pronouncements of economists, once accepted with respect, now elicit ironic responses from a growing band of critics. The reason is obvious. For more than a decade the U.S. economy has been trapped in a state of "stagflation." High-level unemployment has coexisted with a disagreeably high rate of inflation. We have had the worst of both worlds.

From 1963 to 1973 the nation's production of goods and services *per employed worker* grew at an annual rate of 1.9 percent. If that growth rate could have been maintained, the output of goods and services per worker would have doubled in thirty-five years.

After 1973, however, the growth of GNP per employed worker dropped to 0.1 percent per year. If that rate held steady, the output of goods and services per worker *would double in 700 years*. Quite a change. These numbers, which come from the *1980 Economic Report of the President*, reveal an economy rapidly approaching a stationary state.

One of the illusions of modern economics is that this state of affairs is temporary—that we're going through a "difficult transition." One is reminded of the language of science fiction. The relevant analogy is a trip through a "black hole" in outer space. As the space

1

ship approaches the black hole it is rocked by violent turbulence—
everyone aboard becomes totally disoriented. Once sucked through
the black hole—like a soap bubble going down a bathtub drain—the
ship emerges into a new "space" of tranquility. Similarly, in the minds
of today's conventional economists, once we're on the other side of the
terrestrial transition we'll be in a new era of robust economic growth.

The Fundamental Illusion

The *fundamental* illusion of modern economics is that growth is the
answer to all economic problems. The standard argument is that if the
U.S. economy could grow steadily at a *real* rate of, say, 5 percent per
year, inflation, unemployment—and eventually all the problems
associated with wide disparities in income distribution—would
disappear. Of course they would. At that growth rate the nation's
output would double every fourteen years. The most inept political
leaders would find it hard to create economic problems under such
ideal economic conditions. But the *if* in this proposition is a mighty big
one. No economy has ever maintained a *real* growth rate of 5 percent
per year for very long. No economy ever could.

Try to imagine the U.S. economy, which had a Gross National
Product of $2.4 *trillion* in 1979, growing at 5 percent a year, in real
terms, for a century. The result would be $316 trillion worth of output
(in 1979 prices) or 131 times the volume of goods and services
produced in 1979. Even if the American population should triple over
the next century—which isn't likely—this would mean a *44-fold
increase in the output of goods and services per person* by 2079. The
most rabid Utopian couldn't conceive of such cornucopian
abundance.

A corollary of the fundamental illusion is that economic growth
can go on—for practical purposes—forever. No one actually says this
explicitly, and one might be accused of irresponsible hyperbole for
suggesting that anyone even thinks it. But it's implicit in the
prescriptions of conventional economists when addressing contemporary problems.

The Principle of Unlimited Substitutability

The fundamental illusion, and the corollary just mentioned, are based on another major illusion—that scarcity, once the centerpiece of economic analysis, is no longer a problem. The old centerpiece has been replaced by one called the *principle of unlimited substitutability*. The idea of substitution in economic affairs has a very solid basis in theory as well as in fact. Indeed, the ability to substitute one product, process, or resource for another is what makes *any* economic system work. But when the word "unlimited" is added to this principle, it takes on an entirely different meaning. Stripped to its essence, the new principle states that mankind will never run out of anything essential because there will always be a substitute. This process of substitution, the principle asserts, can go on indefinitely.

The principle of unlimited substitutability has an important qualification. It will work only if mankind can find *an unlimited supply of cheap energy*. Clearly, this source of energy won't be fossil fuels. Whether one believes the energy "shortages" of the 1970s were contrived or real, no serious thinker doubts that we'll reach the end of usable fossil fuels someday. We'll never mine the last ton of coal embedded in the bowels of the earth, and we'll never pump the last barrel of oil or the last cubic foot of natural gas. Long before we reach those absolute limits it would take several tons of coal to produce an additional ton; and it would take more than a barrel of oil or a cubic foot of gas to replace themselves. So in real terms—forget money entirely in this context—it no longer will be economically feasible to produce fossil fuels. Before we get to that point, however, those who believe in the principle of unlimited substitutability tell us, we will have achieved a technological breakthrough which will provide the unlimited supply of cheap energy necessary for the principle to work. Then the world will enter the Utopian existence which technological optimists believe is waiting for mankind on the other side of the black hole of "the transition."

There's no mystery about the expected source of unlimited cheap energy. Most of it will be provided, we're told, by nuclear fusion. Without getting into technicalities which would lead us far afield, nuclear fusion means replicating on this planet the conditions that exist at the center of the sun. That would require, of course, something other than earthly matter to "contain" the 100 million degree temperature which nuclear fusion would generate.

The theory of nuclear fusion is well-advanced, and a new branch of physics—plasma physics—has evolved to study the containment of such high temperatures, which thus far have been attained only for a fraction of a second. But there are a lot of unanswered questions about fusion. First, the feasibility of *controlled* fusion remains speculative. Second, while a sustained fusion reaction is theoretically possible, there's no guarantee that the process will produce cheap energy. Fusion power could turn out to be the most expensive power generated by man because no one has the vaguest idea, at this stage of the game, what the capital costs will be. And since the best that can be hoped for is that fusion power will "break even" (that is, that a million Btus of heat generated by the fusion reactor will produce a like amount), some other source of energy—and the only source we know is fossil fuels—will have to be used to produce the machines and other equipment required.

Extremists among the wishful thinkers who believe that nuclear fusion will lead to Utopia view it as a form of perpetual motion. But perpetual motion has eluded mankind thus far, and the laws of physics insure that it will elude us forever.

The principle of unlimited substitutability, with its *total* reliance on unlimited cheap energy, was conceived by physical scientists, not economists. But conventional economists have accepted it and have made it an integral part of their intellectual baggage. Some concept had to take the place of scarcity if their belief that perpetual growth will solve mankind's "transitional" problems is to be sustained.

The attraction of the idea of perpetual growth, and the principles upon which it is based, are obvious. If we can have perpetual growth, those who are relatively well off won't have to share their wealth with others. The "have-nots" of the world—and they number in the billions at the present time—will get their share of a steadily expanding economic pie. As long as they're getting more, we're led to believe, they probably won't fuss too much if the presently well-to-do continue to improve their economic condition.

If we don't have a resumption of economic growth, however—if the "transition" isn't really a transition—if economic conditions get worse rather than better, then all hell is likely to break loose one of these days. And that unhappy day might not be too far down the pike.

It's a truism, but one which conventional economists don't like to think about, that if there is no economic growth, the only way the have-nots can prosper is at the expense of the "haves." Since the poor of the world so greatly outnumber the well-to-do, redistribution of the present stock of the world's real wealth—that is, goods and the capacity to provide services—wouldn't help anyone very much. It's a time-worn cliché, but if we divided everything in the world equally today, we wouldn't be sharing wealth—we'd be sharing the world's poverty.

Illusions and Myths

Illusions provide a fertile breeding ground for myths. There's nothing wrong with myths or fables provided they're recognized as such. The trouble with the myths of modern economics is that they aren't deliberate fabrications. They are firmly believed by many if not most professional economists.

One of the more pervasive myths, although it's not accepted by all economists, is that economics has become a "hard" science. It got that way, the mythmakers believe, by becoming increasingly abstract, and by making extensive use of mathematics. The result is that few of the articles that appear in today's professional journals make any pretense of dealing with reality.

One of the specialized branches of economics is called *econometrics*, an amalgam of economic theory, mathematics, and statistical methods. Econometricians build econometric "models" which may be used for a number of purposes but are used primarily for forecasting. The term "model" might suggest a miniature of reality— there are scale-model airplanes, for example, which differ from their real counterparts only in size. They have to obey the same laws of aerodynamics that real airplanes do or they'll crash. Econometric models, however, are systems of interdependent equations. These equations purport to describe reality, or at least the observable and measurable aspects of reality. But there's no way that an econometric model can be thought of as a small-scale version of the actual economy.

The myth that economics has been converted into a hard science by mathematicization isn't accepted by all economists. John Maynard Keynes and his mentor, Alfred Marshall, two of the greatest names in modern economics, explicitly eschewed the extensive use of mathematics, although both were highly trained in the subject. Wassily Leontief, a Nobel laureate and the founder of a branch of econometrics known as "input-output analysis," has warned against the use of mathematics in ways that trivialize economics rather than making it a "more rigorous" science. William Baumol, another leading American economist, has described some of the attempts to reduce economic issues to arcane symbolism as "illicit intercourse with beautiful models." Like Keynes and Marshall, Leontief and Baumol are skilled mathematicians.

The list could be extended. But the warnings and criticisms of some of the great names in economics have fallen—and continue to fall—on deaf ears. Economics is becoming more, not less, abstract; and it deals less, not more, with issues that are of general concern. If one judges by its professional journals, economics is more rigorous than it used to be. But does that make it more useful? Only in the minds of the mythmakers. Realism and relevance have been sacrificed to rigor. It has been a poor trade-off.

Another myth—not as widespread as the first, but one that seems to be gaining adherents—is that bad news grabs the headlines while the truth (which, of course, is that the news is really good) is ignored. This myth was summarized in an article by Julian Simon, "Resources, Population, Environment: An Oversupply of Fake Bad News" (*Science*, June 27, 1980). He pursued the same theme in another article which appeared in the June 1981 issue of the *Atlantic*. The definitive statement of Simon's Utopian prognosis is given in his 1981 book, *The Ultimate Resource* (Princeton University Press).

Simon lists the headline-grabbing bad news—that there were many deaths due to drought in the Sahel region between 1968-73; that the danger of famine is increasing; that higher population means lower per capita growth; that urban sprawl is reducing "prime" land for agricultural and recreational use; that we're running out of resources; that energy is getting scarcer, and so on. Not so, Simon says. The last two assertions he dismisses out of hand—they don't square with the principle of unlimited substitutability, which Simon clearly accepts without reservation. The other assertions he denies on the grounds that there is no "hard evidence" to back them up.

His own evidence that the world economy is steadily improving is sparse—a few figures here and there, a quotation or two from some source which he considers reliable, and some totally outdated facts. It is anything but convincing. A number of letters by physical and social scientists published in the December 19, 1980, issue of *Science* are highly critical of Simon's methods and conclusions.

In *The Ultimate Resource* Simon argues that the world isn't running out of energy or resources; in fact, they're becoming more abundant. His proof? It requires less labor-time now to produce fossil fuels, minerals, and other resources than it did two centuries, or even a half-century, ago. He has simply restated what every schoolchild knows. Productivity in advanced industrial economies has increased over the past century or two. He doesn't dwell on events of the past decade.

The ultimate resource—the real zinger in Simon's book—is people. The larger the world's population, the better off the world will be. There's no such thing as diminishing returns; there are no diseconomies of scale. The future will always be better than the past, in Simon's view, because mankind has experienced historical progress. So, Simon concludes, there always will be progress.

Garrett Hardin, the distinguished ecologist, has written: "This is not optimism, this is euphoria" (*The New Republic*, October 28, 1981). Hardin notes that "Simon's mind used to be caught in the Malthusian mode and he was 'in the midst of a depression of unusual duration.' He escaped this depression by freeing himself of the Malthusian belief that material limits are real. Now he wants to free others—and to find companions." He wants, in Simon's words, "printer's ink, and research grants for our side." But, Hardin concludes, "Observation shows that printer's ink and research grants (publicity and power) are bestowed in abundance on the Pollyannas of the world. Simon is being greedy when he asks for more than the plethora he has been receiving since he became a born-again optimist.... If the material limits of the world are real ... continued denial of those limits will be disastrous for our descendants."

Do myths such as the one Simon propagates really matter? Can they hurt anyone? If they're harmless, why not indulge them? There's enough bad news in the world, one might argue, without forever harping about the dismal economic future. Unfortunately, the notion that the world economy is steadily improving, and will continue to do so, is not a harmless myth. It perpetuates rampant consumerism in the industrialized nations of the world, and the profligate use of resources and energy, while it does nothing to help the poor and deprived of the world. If most of the residents of the rich and powerful nations of the world believe that future growth will take care of the problems of poverty and deprivation elsewhere, they won't feel any great compulsion to help those who need help right now.

Is there any hope that modern economics will abandon its illusions, that it will once again, as it did during the nineteenth century, deal with reality, even if this means sacrificing some of the rigor and pseudo-scientific mumbo-jumbo which has trivialized a once proud discipline, rather than making it "more scientific"? I think there is, but not as long as economics continues to look inward for signs of progress.

Some of the more remarkable scientific advances of the twentieth century have come from new hybrid disciplines which are amalgams of older sciences formerly kept in jealously-guarded, separate intellectual compartments. DNA, for example, would not have been discovered if Watson and Crick had insisted on remaining within the bounds of a single, narrow "science." And we might still be under the illusion that the atom is infrangible if scientists, mathematicians, and engineers—with widely diversified backgrounds—hadn't been brought together in the Manhattan project. There are many other examples: bio-statistics, geo-statistics, biochemistry, to name only a few. And the integration of the sciences will continue.

Bioeconomics—The Coming Revolution in Economic Thought

There has been one major methodological development in economics which some of us confidently believe will be the wave of the future. It is a development which has attracted considerable attention, and a significant following, in western Europe. But it has been staunchly resisted by the "economics establishment" in this country. It's easy to see why. If the new approach is valid, much of contemporary economics as it is taught and written about in the United States today will have to be scrapped.

The new approach is called "bioeconomics." It is not simply a re-hash of older economic ideas. It is, like some of the new sciences mentioned earlier, a hybrid discipline. It is an amalgam of economic theory, biology, and physics—especially the branch of physics known as thermodynamics. The father of this new hybrid science is Nicholas Georgescu-Roegen, professor emeritus of economics at Vanderbilt University.

A question that puzzles some readers of Georgescu-Roegen's work, as well as that of his interpreters, is: Why is it called "bioeconomics"? The answer is that Georgescu-Roegen views economic development as an extension of natural evolution. All but the simplest species develop *endosomatic* organs which permit them to adapt to a changing environment. The human species is the only one able to develop *exosomatic* organs—tools, weapons, means of transportation, and so forth. This ability has permitted mankind to enjoy the fruits of economic progress. It also is responsible for the problems, economic and ecological, which growth and development have engendered.

A few economists have confused Georgescu-Roegen's system of thought with Edward O. Wilson's sociobiology. It is not necessary to make any judgment about sociobiology to point out that it is completely unrelated to bioeconomics. Both sociobiology and bioeconomics are hybrid disciplines, but that's all they have in common. Sociobiology stresses the genetic determinants of behavior; bioeconomics is concerned with the evolutionary aspects of the economic process. The distinction is more than a semantic one. The two disciplines deal with completely different issues.

Georgescu's early work was traditional, although always orginal and stimulating. But his ideas about the economic process and economic systems evolved steadily. In 1971 Harvard University Press published his book, *The Entropy Law and the Economic Process*, which was soon recognized by perceptive readers as a revolutionary break with the past. In the words of William Nicholls, a former student and himself a distinguished economist, Georgescu advanced the "revolutionary view that economic activity is an extension of man's biological evolution—an entropic process rather than the mechanical analogue traditional in mathematical economics." This is the best concise definition of bioeconomics one can find. But it might help to spell it out in some detail.

Scientific thought evolves in a step-by-step manner. The process of theorizing, which is the essence of scientific thinking, is one of discovering appropriate analogies upon which to build. The differences between conventional economics and bioeconomics—and the analogies on which they're based—can be highlighted by contrasting their essential features.

Conventional Economics—Traditional economics, at least from the days of David Ricardo (1772-1823), has been based on a *mechanistic* model of the economic process. This is illustrated by the circular-flow diagram found on an early page of any comprehensive introductory economics textbook. The circular diagram shows goods flowing in one direction and money (broadly defined) in the other. The point to stress about this diagram is that *the two flows do not alter the system in any way*. A thoughtful student pondering the scheme would be led to observe that (a) it represents a perfectly stationary state, and (b) although time is not mentioned explicitly, the diagram represents perpetual motion.

Bioeconomics—The economic process, according to bioeconomists, is not a mechanistic one. Economic activity is a biological phenomenon, an extension of the process of evolution. Every activity affects the system *in a cumulative manner*. What happens in the economy today will affect the economy tomorrow. The typical economic system goes through a life cycle in terms of *real output per capita*. At first there is slow growth, then growth at an increasing rate. Next, the economy enters the range of diminishing returns. Output per capita increases, but at a diminishing rate. Eventually, the system will reach a state of *absolutely* diminishing returns in which output per capita declines. This doesn't automatically mean catastrophe. Properly managed, an economic system can last for a very long time even under conditions of absolutely diminishing returns.

Conventional Economics—Despite the increased use of mathematics, and the attitude that this has made economics more rigorous, economics remains an inward-looking discipline. Rarely do economists draw on the physical sciences. Even when discussing the economics of energy, many economists display an abysmal ignorance of the physical laws governing the transformation of energy into "work."

Bioeconomics is a genuine hybrid; that is, it is an *amalgam* of economic theory, biology (with its stress on evolution), and thermodynamics. The second law of thermodynamics, the entropy law, is basic to Georgescu-Roegen's system of thought. This law states that there is a *continuous* transformation of energy from its "free" state to a "bound" state. A lump of coal represents "free," or unused, energy. Once it is burned, the energy in that lump of coal has been converted to its bound state. It can never be used again.

Conventional economics is highly compartmentalized. Much contemporary theorizing is completely static; time isn't considered at all. This branch of traditional theory has grown increasingly sterile in recent years. Dynamic analysis, as noted earlier, is basically the economics of growth. The equations used to "describe" the behavior of the economic system in growth models always have exponential solutions. There is a simple reason for this. Growth model builders start with the desired conclusion. They work backwards to derive an equation which projects exponential growth when it is "solved."

Bioeconomics is a unified way of looking at the economic process. The biological analogy which stresses interdependence and evolutionary change is apt. There is no need for the simplifying assumptions of static analysis, or "partial equilibrium." Indeed, the idea of an "equilibrium" or ideal state, in which no change would benefit anyone, is foreign to the philosophy of bioeconomics. Bioeconomists view the economic process as one of continuous change with no predictable endpoint, or ultimate equilibrium, in sight.

Conventional economic theory ignores the supply side of the economic equation. The so-called "new supply side" economics of the 1980s is essentially a resurgence of conservative or "free-market" economics. It is concerned with traditional investment incentives designed to stimulate productivity, which in turn is supposed to lead to a revival of robust economic growth. Energy and raw material supplies are assumed, in effect, to be inexhaustible. As one form of energy or a particular raw material is used up, it will be replaced by another. The problem of energy and resource scarcity is thus assumed away.

Bioeconomics—One of the fundamental propositions of bioeconomics is that all resources are scarce, and that matter as well as energy is subject to "entropic degradation." Some resources can be recycled, but there is necessarily some loss, however infinitesimal, each time they're used. Over a long enough period, pieces of metal (coins, for example) and other substances gradually wear out. The "lost" particles cannot be used again. There is no such thing in bioeconomics as a raw material or other usable substance which is inexhaustible.

There are other differences. But those noted support the earlier assertion that bioeconomics marks a revolutionary break with traditional economics. It is an entirely new way of looking at the economic *process*. Unfortunately, it has disturbing implications. The thought that the world might be close to the apogee of real per capita income is one which traditional economists cannot accept. They know about the law of diminishing returns, but this law is conveniently tucked away in that branch of the discipline called "microeconomics." It applies, they say, to an individual farmer—or any other enterprise with *one fixed* factor of production. But to the world? The thought is too horrible to contemplate. This is exactly the thought, however, that bioeconomists contemplate all the time.

Does it really matter who's right? Economists have always been noted for their squabbles. But who cares? Unfortunately, it does matter. While academic economics has tended to become increasingly abstract, to deal less and less with the real world, a growing number of economists serve as advisers to political, business, labor, and other leaders who are responsible for policies that affect our daily lives. While political policies, in particular, might be far more sensitive to election returns than to the advice of any economist, specific policies show the imprint of economic advisers. Both the White House and Congress have formal economic advisers. And most academic economists are delighted to appear before congressional committees to offer expert (and often contradictory) advice about all matters that have some economic content. There are remarkably few matters that don't.

The advice that conventional economists give is, not surprisingly, very conventional. Even when the current news is bad, conventional economists— influenced by a generation or more of exposure to the "problem-solving" mentality of mathematicians—feel impelled to offer advice on how to convert the present bad news to future good news. Conventional economists remain determinedly optimistic.

The opinions of economists, however, are of more than academic interest. They have an immediate effect on economic behavior and public policy. The Reagan administration's policies, for instance, are based on traditional assumptions. They are entirely demand-oriented.

Will it matter, in the long run, who is right and who is wrong? Unfortunately, it will. Assume for a moment that bioeconomists could convince all the governments of the world that resource scarcity is a serious threat, that unless stringent conservation measures are taken immediately there will be a global catastrophe.

If the governments behaved rationally, they'd take all necessary steps to conserve resources. But let's go on to assume that after a few years it turns out there really is no problem of scarcity. What would happen then? The old growth policies could be reinstated. The policies suggested by bioeconomists, in a word, are entirely reversible. There would be no lasting damage if they were tried and later found to be unnecessary.

Consider the alternative, in which conventional economists continue to influence policy, as they have up to now. Instead of trying to conserve resources, governments would speed up the exploitation of known reserves, and efforts would be made to discover new sources. But suppose that after a few years, or possibly decades, the conventional view turns out to be wrong. The energy consumed will have been converted to heat and dissipated into the atmosphere. The resources used up cannot be replaced. Policies suggested by traditional, demand-oriented principles are, in a word, irreversible. By the time this is discovered, however, it will be too late to turn back. Even a slight change in climate could, at the margin, trigger a catastrophe.

The situation was summed up nicely in a letter to *Science* (December 18, 1980) in which George L. Cowgill, an anthropologist from Brandeis University, commented on Simon's earlier article belittling the scarcity thesis. "It is worth recalling the story of the person who leaped from a very tall building," Cowgill wrote, "and on being asked how things were going as he passed the 20th floor replied, 'Fine, so far.'"

The Shape of the Future—*Global 2000*

In the summer of 1980 the results of a three-year study called *Global 2000* were made public by former Secretary of State Edmund Muskie. The study warns, "World population growth, degradation of the earth's natural resource base, and the spread of environmental pollution, collectively threaten the welfare of mankind." The report provided grim details: The fastest population growth will be in the poorest countries. Better fertilizers and mechanization, needed to increase agricultural productivity, will require more energy. But poor countries won't be able to afford energy from new, "alternative" sources. An estimated 800 million people will go hungry. Forests will disappear, and with them hundreds of species of birds and animals. Clearly, this will threaten the ecological balance of the globe.

The projections of *Global 2000* won't surprise bioeconomists. But in his comments on the report Muskie had the following to say:

"*Global 2000* is not a prediction. If we begin our work now, we will say in twenty years that *Global 2000* was wrong. What a glorious achievement that would be."

How are the potential catastrophes vividly described by the authors of *Global 2000* to be avoided? Simple, according to Muskie. The nations of the world will have to get their economic houses in order. Faster growth will be the order of the day. Alternative sources of cheap energy will have to be discovered, and quickly. Productivity must be increased. The world can't be allowed to reach the state described (but not "predicted") by *Global 2000*.

What will the U.S. and other industrialized nations do to alter present economic behavior patterns? In all likelihood, nothing. That's why it matters whether the world listens to conventional economists or to bioeconomists. If by some strange alchemy industrialized nations could be induced to cooperate in an effort to help the poor of the world, would stimulating more rapid growth "solve" the problem? Far from it. The result might be, in fact, a more serious problem a few years farther along.

For some reason most "long-range" forecasts stop at the year 2000. So the goal becomes one of trying to provide a minimum "decent" standard of living for the billions who will make up the world's poor in that year. But the population won't stop growing in the year 2000. The standard answer to this problem is more and more economic growth. But in any *finite* environment—and the world is finite—there are limits to growth. So perpetual growth can't be the "answer" to the world's economic problems.

How does a bioeconomist respond to *Global 2000*? First, it's a welcome antidote to the flood of blather published and spoken by sincere but misguided futurists who insist there's a Utopia waiting on the other side of the present "difficult transition." Even the press summaries of *Global 2000* should have made any thoughtful observer realize that wishful thinking won't "solve" the economic problems of a world in which population is the only growth variable. Second, let's drop the nonsense that *Global 2000* is not a prediction. It *is* a prediction, whatever its authors intended, and probably a conservative one at that.

So what's the bioeconomic answer to the problem? What basic policy does it suggest? First and foremost is *conservation*. Not just the cosmetic variety we now practice, but a determined effort to avoid waste in all its forms. No amount of preaching will force the well-to-do, spoiled by a quarter-century of rampant consumerism, to practice conservation voluntarily; so it will have to be done by taxation, where that will work, and by even more stringent measures, including rationing, where it won't.

Let's not kid ourselves that the world can feed, house, and clothe another two to three billion persons with no sacrifice on the part of the world's presently industrialized (and prosperous) nations. There will have to be a far more equitable distribution of wealth and income—both within countries like the United States and among the nations of the world—if chaos and localized catastrophe are to be avoided.

Some of the most wasteful practices of rampant consumerism could be eliminated with little more than psychological sacrifice. These include frequent style changes, planned obsolescence, the high costs of hype and other forms of puffery, and needless duplication of many consumer goods—identical in fact, but differentiated in the minds of consumers by brand names and high-powered, expensive advertising. This is not to denigrate the psychic satisfaction engendered by product differentiation. But the time will come when a stable, global social order won't permit such psychic satisfaction for an overfed, overstyled minority while billions elsewhere live on the ragged edge of starvation. Serious conservation of energy and resources, moderate redistribution of wealth and income, and abolition of the excesses of rampant consumerism are diametrically opposed to the growth policies of conventional economics.

Are bioeconomists unaware of technological progress, the *deus ex machina* of conventional economists? Of course not. They believe in it, and they favor it unequivocally and without reservation, provided it is based on a realistic assessment of future energy and resource supplies. Indeed, if disaster is to be avoided the world will need all the technological progress it can muster. But we can have progress—in a meaningful sense—and still do everything possible to eliminate waste.

There's no inconsistency between *reasonable* technological optimism and the bioeconomists' realistic appraisal of the globe's future economic prospects.

There is an inconsistency—in fact, a conflict—between the realistic view of bioeconomists and the mindless optimism engendered by pop-futurists whose excursions into science fiction are offered as serious prognostications. One of the worst offenders in this category is Alvin Toffler, author of the 1980 best seller, *The Third Wave*. As long as a significant proportion of the population remains complacent about the future, such escapes from reality are potentially harmful.

The world can do with a lot less optimism and a great deal more realism. Without realistic leadership in the industrialized nations of the world, there's little hope of radical policy breaks with the past. The revolutionary propositions of bioeconomics indicate that such policy changes have become today's overriding imperatives.

Chapter 2

"NEW" ECONOMICS, OR STALE BEER IN NEW BOTTLES?

The "New" Economics

Is there a "new" economics which will cure stagflation and lead to a revival of economic growth? A number of magazines and newspapers with a conservative bent have created the impression that there is. They regularly publish effusive encomiums about the "new" economists. One of the best-known is Arthur Laffer, who came to prominence during the Nixon years as an adviser to George Shultz, who in turn, held several cabinet offices under Nixon. Laffer is best known for the curve which bears his name. It provides the enlightening information that if taxes were either zero or 100 percent, the economic system would break down. Somewhere in between there's an optimal tax rate which will pay for defense and other necessary public services without diminishing the private incentive to invest. Fortunately, there's more to the "new" economics than this less-than-startling discovery.

The "new" economists want to reduce the role of government in the economy in order to stimulate personal incentive. They believe that government interference in economic affairs has stultified initiative. Inflation and high taxes, they claim, have diminished the public's desire to save and invest. Some want to balance the budget, if not annually, at least over the average business cycle.

18

The "new" economists recognize that today's economic problems, unlike those of the 1930s, are supply- rather than demand-oriented. But they believe all that is needed to stimulate production and efficiency is enhancement of conventional economic incentives. They want the government to permit businesses to make more money and to retain a larger percentage of profits than present tax laws permit.

The message is appealing—particularly to the editors of business-oriented magazines and newspapers. But is it really "new"? Actually, there isn't a thing of substance which the "new" economists say that wasn't said better by Adam Smith in 1776. But the "new" economists live in a world which bears little resemblance to that of 1776.

In *The Wealth of Nations*, Smith attacked the regulations of a system known as Mercantilism. Those regulations favored merchants over manufacturers and workers. They encouraged and legitimized monopolies. Domestic consumption was discouraged so that overseas trade could be maximized. One objective of Mercantilism was to maintain a favorable balance of trade—to export more than the country imported so there would be a steady inflow of gold. This surplus was used to finance overseas military adventures, including the British war against the upstart American colonies.

Smith pointed out that Mercantilism was an extremely inefficient system. If stultifying regulations were abolished, he said, each individual pursuing his self-interest would be "led by an invisible hand to promote an end which was no part of his intention." This end, in today's terminology, would be the largest possible Gross National Product.

Smith's persuasive appeal contributed to the gradual dismantling of Mercantilism. In less than a half-century, Britain moved from rigid controls to *laissez faire* in both domestic and international markets, and Britain prospered as it never had. But this situation didn't last.

If *laissez faire* worked so well in the late eighteenth and early nineteenth centuries, why didn't it survive? And why wouldn't it work today? Smith's prescription worked at a particular time, and in a particular place, but it was not a general principle applicable to all times and all places. As the world changed, *laissez faire* had to be abandoned.

In Smith's day the world was sparsely populated. Most societies were predominantly agrarian. Through a series of lucky accidents, Great Britain took the lead in industrialization. It colonized and controlled vast "backward" areas of the earth, and it completely dominated the world's oceans both militarily and commercially. This unbalanced world proved to be unstable. The American colonies broke away, starting the dissolution of the Empire. After our own Civil War, the U.S. took the lead in industrialization and economic growth.

The system of essentially unrestrained capitalism worked well in the United States until 1929. One of the consequences, however, was a badly skewed distribution of wealth and income. This resulted in a decline in the "marginal propensity to consume," in the words of the great British economist J. M. Keynes, as well as a diminution of the inducement to invest.

The British economy slid into a depression in the early 1920s which lasted until rearmament started in the late 1930s. The U.S. economy held off until 1929, when it too was plunged into a depression. In 1935 Keynes published his classic *General Theory of Employment, Interest and Money.* He argued that the chronic unemployment which had plagued industrialized nations during the interwar period could be cured only by maintaining "aggregate effective demand." Keynes explained why aggregate demand in mature capitalist societies had failed to keep pace with economic growth. Advancing technology had increased the capacity of the system to produce an ever-expanding volume of goods and services. There was no shortage of desire for those goods and services on the part of the working population. But desire has to be backed by purchasing power before it becomes demand. Purchasing power, however, was unequally distributed, and the rich could consume only so much.

As the volume of plant and equipment increased, the return on investment declined. This, in turn, reduced the inducement to invest amounts sufficient to maintain full employment. The government, Keynes said, would have to encourage the expansion of investment *and consumption* so that full employment equilibrium could be restored. This would be done by direct investment in public works and by what later came to be called expansionist monetary and fiscal policies.

The economies that had suffered chronic depression in the 1920s and 1930s experienced remarkable revivals as they geared up for, and later became involved in, World War II. Military spending and armed conflict were not what Keynes had in mind. But the economic *effects* of the war were considered by many to be a vindication of Keynes's *General Theory*. World War II required enormous investments in plant and machinery, and the consumption of the armed forces was so great that rationing was required in the civilian sector to insure a relatively equitable distribution of goods and services not consumed directly by the war effort.

Many economists expected a return to the pre-war depression following the end of hostilities. But the world's mature economies had started to change even before the start of World War II, and they continued to change afterwards. The old system of *laissez-faire* capitalism was gone. In its place were systems called, somewhat inelegantly, "mixed economies." These remained basically capitalistic; the means of production were still owned and operated by private enterprises. But central governments were no longer passive partners in the economic process. Governments influenced the level—and to some extent the direction—of economic activity, primarily through a variety of monetary and fiscal policies.

It appeared, particularly during the 1960s, that the ideal balance between private and public involvement in the operation of the economy had been found. The 1960s were the Golden Age of the "mixed" economic systems which had evolved during and after World War II. It was a decade of virtually uninterrupted economic growth in the United States. And during the first half of that decade, unemployment rates were low while prices were relatively stable. As noted at the beginning of Chapter 1, real output per worker increased by almost 2 percent per year. Economists confidently believed that these ideal conditions could be maintained indefinitely by minute adjustments in monetary and fiscal policy, or "fine tuning" as they called it. But the era of robust economic growth ended in the late 1960s. Most economists, and most of the public, haven't accepted this unpleasant fact despite the steadily mounting evidence which supports it.

The "new" economists aren't as different from their conventional brethren as their admirers imply. U.S. economists are overwhelmingly conservative. The "new" economists are just more conservative than others. Like most economists today, they ignore the ubiquitous law of diminishing returns. This law—not the duplicity and cupidity of businessmen and politicians—explains the rising costs of energy and raw materials.

Not all laymen are gulled by the "new" economics. In a letter to the Sunday *New York Times* (August 26, 1979), Joseph A. Linsk of Atlantic City, N.J.—who I assume is not an economist—said the following: The way out of our difficulties is to develop "an American lifestyle which will finally say no to the glut—stop driving, stop cooling, stop heating, stop sucking, chewing and gorging on such an inordinate share of the earth's wealth. Not driving when you can walk, not stupidly freezing in over air-conditioned lounges, not lighting unused rooms, playing unwatched TV sets, toasting in needless heat— these are the ukases to be preached from the citadels of power, from TV stations, newspapers, boardrooms, etc."

There is more wisdom in these words than in the aggregate lucubrations of the scores of economists whose arcane papers fill the pages of the profession's leading journals each year. In those papers, economists appear to be far more intent on impressing one another with their virtuosity than in dealing with the slowly worsening condition of the global economy.

Supply-Side Economics

Some business writers use the term "supply-side" economics to distinguish the "new" economists from those who continue to insist that the country is suffering from a lack of aggregate demand.

Supply-side concerns, according to one business-oriented publication, include "commodity shortages, slow productivity growth, sluggish capital investment, inadequate manufacturing capacity, and regulation" (*Business Week*, September 17, 1979). It also mentions in passing, but does not dwell on, "resource shortages." There's not an item on this list, however, that is new.

The author of the *Business Week* article maintained that a major problem of supply-side economics is that it lacks a unifying theory such as that provided by Keynes for demand-side economics. There is a unifying supply-oriented theory. But it is a major departure from traditional economics, and since conventional economists have not been able to refute it—or to challenge the analytical methods used—most of them have ignored it.

The only supply-oriented theory that can legitimately be called new is the one advanced by Georgescu-Roegen. Conventional economists, whether they stress the demand side or the supply side, view the economic system as a vast machine. It's a strange machine, however, which not only needs replacement parts on a regular basis but has to grow continuously if it is to run properly. Keynesians, Neo-Keynesians, and the "new" supply-side economists all have a common objective: By one means or another, get the economy growing again.

Bioeconomists view the economic system in an entirely different way. They see it as an organism, and like any other organism it goes through a life cycle. At first the system grows slowly. Later, it enters a period of more rapid, self-sustaining growth. As the system reaches maturity, it grows very slowly again, or not at all. Still later, the economic system will begin to wind down. Eventually, like every other organism, it will cease to exist.

A few conventional economists have tried to discredit bioeconomics by lumping it with "doomsday" theories. That could be an honest misinterpretation, based on inadequate understanding, or it could be an attempt to protect outmoded ideas in which—through their writing and teaching—they have a vested interest. Most, however, continue to ignore this new paradigm.

The worst interpretation that can be put on Georgescu-Roegen's views is that he believes the end of the world is at hand, so all that remains is "to flee to the hills." Just as economic growth was a long, slow process covering centuries, the process of "winding down" can be long and slow. The decline can be controlled. To accommodate to economic decline, however, will require a different set of policies than those advocated by conventional economists, who believe that faster growth is the only solution to our problems.

Bioeconomists urge policies that will force conservation of the world's dwindling endowment of energy and natural resources. They place more emphasis on an equitable distribution of goods and services than do conventional economists. They also recognize the need for steady progress on the technological front, perhaps even more than their conventional brethren. The "winding down" phase of the world economy can be stretched only by using our scarce resources more efficiently in the future than we have in the past.

Zero-Sum Games

One of the most highly publicized books by an economist to appear in recent years was *The Zero-Sum Society* (Basic Books, 1980) by Lester C. Thurow of MIT. Its paperback edition became a best seller in 1981. The title derives from the notion of a zero-sum game, such as a neighborhood poker game, in which total losses equal total winnings. The idea was first applied to economic problems in the 1940s by John von Neumann, one of the great mathematicians of this century, and Oskar Morgenstern, an economist. It's been used since then in a variety of contexts by economists and others.

Thurow examines a number of economic problems in a political context. "Technologically," he wrote, "energy independence is well within our reach. Politically, it may not be within our reach at all." Efforts to deregulate trucking—which Thurow thinks would have widespread, favorable repercussions—encounter opposition from trucking firms and Teamsters and are thus frustrated. Deregulation of trucking, in his view, would lead to aggressive competition and lower prices for all products affected by transportation costs. Other objectives which Thurow regards as economically desirable cannot overcome political opposition.

Thurow is regarded as a political "liberal." But he has an implicit faith in the efficacy of price competition. On this score, the distance between Thurow and Milton Friedman strikes me as being short. In an earlier day, Thurow says, powerful economic groups could gain at the expense of the powerless. Gains weren't offset by losses because "the losses were allocated to particular powerless groups rather than spread across the population." Now, minority groups are unwilling to accept further losses.

Is Thurow suggesting a return to the earlier uneven distribution of power? Not at all. The policies he proposes are a curious mixture of *laissez faire* and increased government intervention. The business community would warmly welcome the former; liberals and radicals would welcome the latter. One would have to suffer from ideological schizophrenia, however, to accept the entire package.

Some of the specifics in Thurow's policy package are deregulation of energy prices and elimination of the corporate income tax. Underlying the first is the assumption that vigorous competition would add to energy supplies. Rising corporate profits, meanwhile, would attract huge investments to stimulate increased productivity and the return of economic growth. But Thurow hedges his bets. He also wants the government to invest heavily in growth industries and to guarantee jobs for everyone. On the one hand he wants to reduce tax collections, but on the other he wants government to increase spending to achieve full employment.

Thurow's book was warmly received by liberal and radical economists. Some were skeptical about his policy recommendations, but one reviewer has hailed his book as "an elegantly reasoned interpretation of American economic troubles." Another described Thurow as "idealistic and pragmatic, academic and commonsensical."

The Zero-Sum Society contains a number of insights, although most can be found in the earlier writings of John Kenneth Galbraith. What is surprising is that reviewers haven't been struck by the incongruity of his policy proposals. And one does not have to assume that present American economic policies are internally consistent to feel that Thurow's proposals are not.

A major disappointment in *The Zero-Sum Society* is its total reliance on conventional economics. Some of Thurow's admirers may have confused felicitous prose with fresh analytical insights. One doesn't have to look too hard to see that both the diagnoses and prescriptions are based on traditional, demand-oriented economic theory. Thurow believes we could solve our economic problems by rational political behavior. Like others who ignore energy and resource constraints, he sees our problems as man-made and thus susceptible to man-made solutions.

One commentator suggested that Thurow will be the leading guru of a social democratic movement which that commentator is certain will emerge in the near future. His vision, however, is clouded. Like it or not, the only trend most political analysts see today is one of growing conservatism. It's hard to imagine either democratic socialists or Reagan-type conservatives accepting Thurow as their guru. A policy package that stretches from one end of the political spectrum to the other will probably end up appealing to no one. Although Thurow's policy package might not beguile anyone in a position to implement it, the appeal of his book is understandable. It has a problem-solving orientation. In an age when economic and social problems abound, problem solvers find a receptive audience. Before returning to this issue, however, a book which made an even bigger splash than Thurow's will be discussed briefly.

Adam Smith Redivivus

George Gilder's popular book, *Wealth and Poverty* (Basic Books, 1981), is one of a long line of spirited defenses of "capitalism," a system which, Gilder asserts, is thoroughly believed in only by those who have never experienced it.

A defense requires an opponent, if only a straw man. Gilder's is what he calls "socialism," although it's a strange opponent because his book opens with the sentence: "The most important event in the recent history of ideas is the demise of the socialist dream." Still, the socialist dream—like the proverbial dead horse—is flayed mercilessly.

Wealth and Poverty is an unusual collection of ancient apothegms and ideas newly defined to suit Gilder's purposes. The old stuff has been presented so often, and so much better, by Milton Friedman and his followers, that it must be well known by now. Much of the new material, including some which excited reviewers, beggars belief.

What the United States has to do, in Gilder's view, is "overcome the materialist fallacy; the illusion that resources and capital are essentially things, which can run out, rather than products of human will and imagination which in freedom are inexhaustible. This fallacy is one of the oldest of economic delusions, from the period of mercantilism when they fancied it was gold, to the contemporary period when they suppose it is oil; and our citizens clutch at real estate and gold as well."

Mr. Gilder doesn't know his economic history very well. The Mercantilists were never under the illusion that gold was "wealth." They knew, however, that gold was scarce and a universally acceptable medium of exchange. They also knew that by maintaining a "favorable balance of trade" they could accumulate gold which was used to finance colonial expansion. Gilder slanders the Mercantilists, however, when he implies they believed that gold itself possessed utility.

That's a trivial point when one examines the rest of the above quotation. In Gilder's view resources and capital aren't tangible—they aren't real. They're figments of the imagination, and we can, of course, imagine an inexhaustible number of things. We will never, therefore, run out of resources or capital.

How does Gilder reach this conclusion? What evidence does he adduce to support it? Simple. Germany and Japan aren't heavily endowed with resources, but they have "free minds." Gilder doesn't try to convince us that the Germans and Japanese "imagine" resources. Their free minds allow them to get the resources they don't have, fabricate them, and sell them at a profit in world markets.

The stories of Japanese and West German economic growth have been repeated so often that there can be few Americans who don't know them. But the explanation is also common knowledge. Both economies started almost from scratch thirty-five years ago, with substantial American help. When they got back into production they used the latest designs in plant and equipment. They easily out-produced the U.S., Great Britain, and others hindered by older plant and equipment.

What is not so well-known, and a point Gilder doesn't mention since it would interfere with his plot, is that growth rates have declined in Germany and Japan, as they have throughout the industrial world. It's taking the Japanese and the West Germans a bit longer to encounter diminishing returns, but they're getting there.

The idea that the U.S. should emulate West Germany and Japan has become almost a fetish in some conservative circles. Certainly we should learn everything we can from them. But Gilder's basic premise—that resources and capital aren't real—cannot be taken seriously. He maintains that the notion that resources are finite is a "socialist" one. That is why, Gilder asserts, socialists have a limited view of the future. Socialists of all persuasions, however, take exactly the opposite view. They are Utopians who believe the only thing that stands between mankind and permanent prosperity is the institution of private property.

Socialists would be quick to agree with Gilder that contemporary economic problems are the result of human institutions and human error. Neither the socialists nor Gilder would be willing to consider the proposition that the world's economic problems are due to biological and thermodynamic causes. Both would assert that these problems are man-made and hence susceptible to human solution. Although they're at opposite poles of the political spectrum, both Gilder and the socialists he attacks so vigorously are problem-solvers.

Problem-Solving

"Why can't a nation which sent a man to the moon solve its ___ problem?" Insert (a) inflation, (b) unemployment, (c) pollution, (d) energy, or (e) any other current social or economic problem, and you'll recognize a statement you've seen or heard before.

Why should a nation with as many technical achievements to its credit as the United States be plagued by a host of annoying, and seemingly intractable, problems? This question stems from a failure to distinguish between technical and social problems.

When President Kennedy and Congress agreed to put a man on the moon before 1970, a clear-cut goal was established. Funds were appropriated, and NASA was given the go-ahead to solve the technical problems involved. The rest is history. The problems were solved by a massive scientific and engineering effort.

Why can't we just as easily "solve" other problems, such as the energy problem, by a similar approach? There are many reasons, but one of the more important is that not everyone agrees there is an energy problem. If we can't agree there's a problem, how could anyone come up with a generally acceptable solution? The scientists who worked on the moon trip didn't haggle about alternate routes or whether the trip should be by rocket, ship, or car. They dealt with a limited number of variables. They had a single objective. While they richly deserve credit for the successful moon shot, they were dealing with a problem that is simple compared with the economic problems of a democratic society.

Consider the problem of inflation. No one publicly denies that a problem exists. But the number of proposed "solutions" equals the number of major pressure groups in our society. Some advocate a curb on wage increases but would allow market forces to determine product and service prices. A few have called for overall price and wage controls. Others have proposed an "incomes" policy which would try to maintain the relative shares received by each major group of income recipients.

Economists don't agree about the causes of or cures for inflation. Prices are determined by the forces of supply and demand. But those forces are numerous and complex. Some economists emphasize supply forces, such as negotiated wage increases. Others insist that demand forces, such as the money supply, are of primary importance. The policies advocated by these two groups are widely different.

We never would have had a man on the moon if scientists and engineers had been unable to agree on a definition of the problem. There is no disagreement among economists about basic principles— on this score economists are as "scientific" as physicists. But economics is not a "value-free" science, as physics and chemistry are. The proposals advanced by economists are colored—consciously or unconsciously—by their notions about the kind of society they consider to be best. Some economists find controls totally objectionable; others do not. Some are primarily concerned about the effects of public policy on efficiency; others are more concerned about equity or the way income is distributed.

There is another major difference between the moon trip and economic problems. The moon trip was a single problem that was handled in isolation. It didn't have to be solved in conjunction with a host of other engineering problems. But economic problems are not independent of one another. Inflation, for example, is related to energy problems, unemployment, and resource scarcities. It is also related to the size and composition of the federal budget, urban problems, and a long list of others.

Many scientific and engineering problems come as neatly tied packages. There is no partial solution. The problem is solved or it isn't. Most social and economic problems, however, are interrelated. To "solve" one might exacerbate another.

The public isn't well served by political leaders who talk about "solving" this or that economic or social problem. There is a great need for better public understanding of the complexity and interdependence of such problems as inflation, unemployment, urban blight, energy shortages, and so forth. Improved communication between economists and the public won't solve the problems, but it could help in the process of accommodation to a changing world in which new problems seem to appear faster than we are able to learn to live with old ones.

Knowledge and Belief

A friend who is a physical scientist claims he's found the difference between the "hard sciences"—physics, chemistry, etc.—and economics. The hard sciences, he maintains, are based on knowledge; economics is based on belief. That's why, he maintains, economists can't give lawmakers useful advice on how to deal with the country's multiplying economic problems.

To some extent he's right. He would be wrong, of course, if he suggested that everything in the physical sciences is cut and dried. He's aware, however, that there are points of disagreement among physicists, chemists, and especially biologists. It's equally important to point out that there are basic principles on which economists agree completely, regardless of which school of thought they belong to. Knowledge implies certainty, however, while belief implies uncertainty, and there is more uncertainty in economics than in the hard sciences. This will no doubt always be so.

There is a fundamental difference between the "raw materials" used in the physical and the social sciences. Molecules, protons, and neutrinos don't express opinions—their behavior doesn't affect lawmakers' decisions. The more physicists, chemists, and biologists learn about the composition of matter, living and inert, the better they can predict the outcomes of physical, chemical, and biological changes.

Social scientists, however, deal with the most unpredictable elements in the universe—men and women. Not only is their behavior unpredictable; it's often perverse, from a social point of view. Also, the conclusions economists reach about economic policies are influenced by their personal values—by the individual economist's ideas about the kind of society he or she thinks would be best.

If economic conclusions are influenced by individuals' values, why is economics ever referred to as a "science"? There's no reason why it shouldn't be. "Science" isn't concerned with objects; it's concerned with method. One can be just as scientific studying human behavior as in the study of inert matter. The important thing isn't the subject being studied but the way in which it is studied.

Slopping around in a chemistry laboratory, mixing substances at random, isn't science. Neither is using a set of numbers to support a predetermined conclusion while ignoring other numbers that would deny that conclusion. But two equally competent economists can work with the same data and arrive at different policy recommendations. This is partly because the complexity of economic problems guarantees there won't be a unique solution. It's partly because different economists have different ideas about what constitutes the best society.

One economist might believe that every individual is entitled to retain as much income as possible. That economist might recommend flat percentage taxes. Another economist, with equal sincerity, might hold a different view about the appropriate distribution of a nation's output, and advocate steeply progressive taxes. The two have different notions of what constitutes a "fair" distribution of income and output. And fairness is one of the things for which there is not—and never will be—a scientific test.

The advocate of a proportionate tax might claim it is necessary for some individuals to accumulate wealth to invest in productive facilities which provide jobs. The supporter of progressive taxation might counter that income inequality will lead to underconsumption and fewer jobs. Both know the theoretical underpinnings of each other's arguments; there's no uncertainty involved. But the two differ in their evaluation of the consequences of each type of tax system. This is a matter of belief.

When economists are criticized for failing to agree on policy matters, their critics fail to recognize that disagreement is one consequence of a democratic society. In a totalitarian state, economists agree on all policy matters—at least in public. The essence of a democratic society is diversity, and diversity breeds disagreement. This makes it hard for democratic societies to deal with serious problems such as the energy situation and persistent inflation.

When lawmakers fail to act forthrightly, by trying to find a "workable compromise," their failure is more often due to belief than to knowledge. Economists know, for example, that comprehensive, mandatory wage and price controls would halt the upward spiral of prices. But many believe that this solution would create other problems—black markets and excessive bureaucracy—which they consider to be as bad as inflation.

Black markets can be controlled. And reasons are given in the next chapter why there wouldn't have to be a massive bureaucracy to administer wage and price controls—or the rationing which such controls would require. But the dominant belief is the opposite one. As long as it remains the dominant belief, we can expect no relief from inflation.

Theory Versus Practice

Few words are more often used incorrectly in popular discussion of scientific matters than "theory." For example: "Oh, sure, that's fine in theory, but it won't work in practice." That statement makes no sense. If something won't work in practice, it's not fine in theory. The theory behind it is useless and should be abandoned.

If something works, however, we assume it's soundly grounded in theory, although the theory might not be "perfectly general." Wilbur and Orville Wright developed a theory of flight and went on to build successful flying machines. Their theory has been modified, expanded, and made more general. But it's still not perfect.

According to the traditional theory of flight, a bumble bee—with its body and wing configuration—will never get off the ground. Bumble bees not only fly, however, they fly extremely well. They hover, zoom, climb, and dive at incredible speeds. They're more efficient flying machines than man-made aircraft. But in principle they ought to be grounded.

Should we abandon the existing theory of flight? Of course not. It has produced a vast array of specialized flying machines that work well. We just have to admit that the theory of flight isn't perfectly general, and generality is the ultimate goal of all theorists. Few laymen are likely to discuss the theory of flight. But many discuss economic matters since these impinge on our daily lives. In these discussions theory is often misused as an antonym for "practical."

Thomas Robert Malthus, whose name is generally associated with the idea of overpopulation, was aware of how practical persons regarded theorists. At the Malthus centennial celebration in 1935, J. M. Keynes quoted Malthus:

We are continually hearing declamations against theory and theorists by men who pride themselves upon . . . being practical. . . . Bad theories are bad things, and the authors of them useless, and sometimes pernicious members of society. But these advocates of practice do not seem to be aware that they themselves very often come under this description, and that a great part of them may be classed among the most mischievous theorists of their time. (*Economic Journal*, June 1935).

Malthus noted that practical persons often generalize on the basis of their personal experience—the worst kind of theorizing.

Economic theories don't grow in a vacuum. They're a response to economic problems. The theorist hopes that by stating the problem in a simplified and abstract form its causes can be identified. If the theory is plausible, it might suggest one or more methods of coping with the problem.

The problem that troubled the industrial world in the 1930s was massive, persistent unemployment. Keynes said it was caused by inadequate demand for capital and consumer goods. The proposed solution? Stimulate investment and consumer spending. World War II showed Keynes to be right. But he was overambitious when he called his theory a general one. It was the correct response to depression. But it's purely a theory of demand—supply is taken for granted. So it's far from general.

The only theory that addresses today's problems adequately is Nicholas Georgescu-Roegen's bioeconomic theory. It will take political leaders longer to recognize the correctness of Georgescu's views than it did for Keynes's ideas to be accepted. Most politicians didn't accept "Keynesianism" until after his theory was no longer useful. Since 1969 the problems that have baffled political leaders, as well as traditional economists, have been supply problems. Stimulating demand won't alleviate them.

One of Keynes's lasting contributions is a statement in his *General Theory* about the tenacity of ideas. Old ideas, he wrote, are hard to shake. He expected it would be a long time before his new idea would be accepted. Keynes's dictum about the tenacity of ideas is still true. This is why political leaders are unable to cope with today's intractable economic problems. They're trying to attack supply problems with policies based on demand theory. A new supply theory has been formulated by Georgescu-Roegen but it is not yet widely accepted. He is probably a generation ahead of his time.

Useful theories eventually produce practical results. Einstein's theories ultimately led to the atomic bomb and nuclear power. Today's computers are a result of mathematical theorizing by Norbert Weiner and John von Neumann. We might easily have slipped back into a post-war depression had it not been for Keynes's theory. Not every theory, however, is useful. Those that aren't eventually fall by the wayside.

When laymen refer to an economist as a "theorist," they use the term in a pejorative sense. The intellectual leaders of any scholarly community, however, are its theorists. The layman's intent might be a put-down. In fact, it will be interpreted as the ultimate compliment.

Chapter 3

THE HEART OF THE MATTER: ENERGY AND ITS DISCONTENTS

Energy Shortage: Fact or Fiction?

It's widely believed that the "energy crisis" started when world oil prices doubled in 1974. But the *real* price of oil—the ratio of petroleum prices to all-commodity prices—which had been declining slowly for some time, jumped sharply in 1969. That, significantly, was the year which marked the end of robust economic growth, not only in the United States but in most industrial nations. The economic news since then has been consistently bad, although some periods have been worse than others. It's been a long time since anyone could produce good economic news and back up the announcement with solid facts. What is surprising is that in spite of the dismal record of the past decade, the majority of economists continue to be optimistic about the long-run future.

Some scientists say there aren't now—and never will be—real shortages of anything. Economists are receptive to this line of thinking. The principle of unlimited substitutability, referred to in Chapter 1, was developed by H. E. Goeller and Alvin M. Weinberg, of the Oak Ridge National Laboratory, in an article published in the December 1978 issue of *The American Economic Review*.

What is the Goeller-Weinberg message? In a nutshell, it's that "institutional deficiencies," not actual physical scarcity, are the cause of present (and future) problems. In other words, if we can only learn to behave rationally, the marketplace will take care of everything else. There is one caveat in their argument, however. All the good things they predict will happen, they state in their article, only if "man finds an inexhaustible, non-polluting source of energy." And this, as a moment's reflection makes clear, is a pretty important cautionary remark.

Statements like those made by Goeller-Weinberg—echoed by Julian Simon and who knows how many other economists and technological optimists—keep the public confused on the energy issue. Not all scientists agree with them, of course. But the technological optimists keep shouting down those who disagree with their position. The public—not understanding the technical and economic complexities involved—always prefers good news to bad. And this preference, among other things, stands in the way of an effective national energy policy.

There have been two distinct cycles in the global oil market since 1973, and this pattern is likely to be repeated in the future. The U.S., as the world's dominant energy consumer, has had a major influence on these cycles.

The average price paid by U.S. refiners for all crude oil (domestic and imported) rose from less than $5 per barrel in 1973 to $10 by 1975. Average consumption, meanwhile, dropped by almost one million barrels a day. This was followed by a drop in world oil production from 1974 until mid-1975. But prices rose slowly from 1975 to 1978, and U.S. consumption picked up smartly—going from about 16.2 to almost 19 million barrels a day. World production turned up again. From the cyclical low of about 54 million barrels daily it rose to a new peak of nearly 64 million in 1978.

The second round started in 1978. The average U.S. refinery price for all crude jumped from $12 per barrel that year to $28 by 1980, making the 1974 price increase seem mild by comparison. Daily consumption in the U.S. dropped below the 1973 level, and world production was curtailed once again. By 1980, output was down to an estimated 55 million barrels a day.

The spot market price for Arabian light crude declined from $42 per barrel in November 1980 to $32 in June 1981. The latter was below the official OPEC benchmark price of $34 per barrel. The bellweather spot market price convinced many observers—and the public at large—that there was a world oil glut, although relatively little crude oil was being traded on the spot market. The uninitiated saw this as a harbinger of a major drop in retail gasoline prices.

There were a few reductions in wholesale oil prices during the first half of 1981, but there was nothing resembling a general price reduction. Price cuts reflected the reduction of premiums added to the basic OPEC price during the earlier period of rising consumption and increasing prices. They represented a "readjustment," not a significant reduction.

As the glut persisted into 1982, however, there were further modest price reductions, by both OPEC and non-OPEC producers. In March 1982, for example, Mexico—which does not belong to OPEC—cut its prices by as much as $2.50 a barrel. Some OPEC producers, meanwhile, were "shading" prices by offering easier credit terms or making other concessions, which effectively brought the price below the official $34 per barrel. There was a special effort by OPEC officials to stimulate purchases of oil from Nigeria, where, in April 1982, daily production was running at about 62 percent of its assigned OPEC ceiling.

Throughout the glut of the early 1980s there was speculation in the press about the possibility of a cut in OPEC's official benchmark price. As late as April 1982, however, the cartel had managed to hold the line. By then, spot prices had stabilized, and modest declines in U.S. gasoline prices were tapering off. OPEC survived the glut by imposing a daily production ceiling of 17.5 million barrels. By contrast, in 1979 OPEC countries were producing at a rate of 31 million barrels a day.

By a disciplined response, OPEC survived the glut of the early 1980s, as it had the earlier glut of 1977. In spite of this, writers whose stock in trade is wishful thinking—or in some cases xenophobia—continued to express the hope that even if the cartel's back hadn't been broken it had been at least seriously weakened.

Breaking Up OPEC—Premature Obituaries

After the 1973-74 oil embargo there was a spate of articles by economists predicting the "impending breakup of OPEC." It would happen, they alleged, because cartels are "inherently unstable." Those economists seemed unable to distinguish between the abstract models of economics textbooks and the real world.

Their reasoning was simple. Higher energy prices would lead to a sharp drop in demand. The cartel would be caught with an oversupply. Individual members, motivated by greed, would start to shade prices. The first price drop would invite retaliation, which would set off a full-scale price war. The foundations of the cartel would crumble; it would soon be no more. World oil prices would fall back to $1.50 a barrel. Gasoline prices would decline, and we'd all live happily ever after.

This sounds plausible enough. Why didn't it happen? Several reasons. Oil prices increased sharply after the embargo, consumers did cut their gasoline purchases, and there was a slight oil surplus for a brief period. But did the individual members of the cartel react as they were supposed to? No. The discipline of the cartel held firm. Instead of cutting prices, the members cut production. Meanwhile, American consumers became accustomed to higher prices and soon guzzled gasoline more wildly than ever. This continued through successive rounds of moderate price increases. In spite of the much larger price increases that took place between 1978 and 1980, most energy economists were remarkably reticent about the instability of OPEC.

When the energy economists' earlier predictions failed to materialize, they quietly faded into the background. Others—mostly journalists—leaped into the breach. Ironically, the authorities they cited were the same economists whose forecasts were so wide of the mark after the first round of major price increases.

In the January 1979 issue of *Harper's*, for example, Craig Karpel, a journalist and executive director of the nonprofit Council on Energy Policy, Inc., described "Ten Ways to Break OPEC." Knowingly or not, he made the same assumptions as the economists who earlier had predicted OPEC's demise. The key assumption is that there's an unlimited supply of oil in the United States; all we have to do is find it.

Anyone who believes this can easily believe the rest of the article, despite its disregard of facts.

Articles such as Karpel's are harmless. They simply rehash outdated notions that no one will take seriously. Ludicrous as his proposals are, they aren't the silliest to be advanced. The head of one of the country's largest conglomerates claimed that OPEC is violating U.S. antitrust laws. He's right, of course. There also might be individuals in some OPEC countries who ignore our anti-polygamy laws. They're certainly not paying any attention to American laws regarding compulsory education. Indeed, the residents of an OPEC country might be forgiven for asking: "Why do you think your laws apply to us?"

The proposal to take OPEC to court for restraint of trade had the support of the International Association of Machinists, which, some business groups say, "violates" the antitrust laws every day. The proposal also had the backing of Senator Daniel Patrick Moynihan.

Not all proposals to wreck OPEC are harmless. Chauvinists and xenophobes stalk the land. Right-wing commentators talk about OPEC's "war on the democracies." This kind of talk naturally begets proposals to wage war on the cartel. Not conventional war. Even the wildest chauvinist knows the United States couldn't get away with a military takeover of any major oil-exporting country without provoking retaliation. What then? The "letters" columns of business-oriented publications abound with suggestions. Many drip venom toward foreigners who have the unmitigated gall to interfere with our driving pleasure.

At least one economist remained intransigent, demanding a confrontation with OPEC. Paul Davidson, of Rutgers University, was quoted in *Business Week* (June 25, 1979) as saying that we've been asked to "learn to live with the cartel by starving to death. The policy should be to fracture OPEC." He offered no specific suggestions, but such proposals sound warlike. Davidson evidently agrees with those victims of xenophobia who believe it is "our" oil which OPEC is withholding from the insatiable American consumer. He also exaggerated inordinately when he suggested that living with the cartel will result in "starvation."

One proposal called for the formation of a countercartel of oil-importing nations to withhold food, equipment, and other exports to OPEC countries. This suggestion assumes that the importers' cartel would be as disciplined as that of the exporters. But Japan, for example, gets more then 90 percent (as opposed to our 50 percent) of its oil from OPEC. It can't risk a shutdown. Neither could Western European countries. Unless we were prepared to go to total regulation "for the duration," neither could the United States.

Where does that leave us? What can we do? Exactly what former Energy Secretary James Schlesinger—and his former deputy, John F. O'Leary—told us repeatedly we had to do. Curb our gasoline appetites. The pricing mechanism has done this to a limited extent. Eventually, however, we will have to turn to rationing. This proposal, which assumes we will want to deal with the energy problem rationally, is discussed later.

The Windfall Oil Tax: Misguided Solution to a Misunderstood Problem

The windfall oil tax bill was signed by President Carter on April 2, 1980. At the signing ceremony, the president referred to the new law as "the keystone of our energy policy." That was the sort of judgment which led the devout to pray and non-believers to seek solace in whatever best diverted their attention from the world around them.

The windfall profits tax was a response to public frustration. American consumers had been spoiled by an abundance of cheap gasoline. Suddenly, gasoline was hard to get. When the pipelines began to empty, fuel prices shot up faster than other prices which already were wrecking the typical family's budget. Someone had to be punished for those heinous crimes against rampant consumerism.

The trouble is that the windfall profits tax didn't punish the individuals who run the oil companies. The companies themselves, while legal entities, are pure abstractions which feel no pain. Neither oil company executives nor their employees suffered pay cuts as a result of the law. Dividends might or might not have been affected. That depended on how the managers of oil companies wanted the public to view this punitive and discriminatory tax. It definitely meant that oil companies would have less to invest in alternative energy sources—including coal gasification and liquefaction.

There are several things this "keystone policy" did not do. It did not add significantly to the nation's energy supply. It did not slow the rising energy price spiral. By itself, it didn't stimulate conservation. It did not, in brief, alter behavior patterns which might have helped the nation adapt to a new era of chronic energy scarcity.

Part of the $288 billion which the tax was expected to add to the public coffers during the 1980s would have been collected anyway. Even with a fixed percentage limit on corporate taxes, the amount of tax collected goes up as total profits increase.

Doesn't the windfall profits tax have any redeeming features? It did authorize $3.1. billion from the general fund to help low-income families. A rider provided modest tax exemptions on dividends and interest, approximately $4.3 billion, as a *quid pro quo* for the middle class. The poor, as we know, rarely get income from stocks, bonds, or savings. One effect which most commentators overlooked at the time was that the law took the heat off the oil companies. They were duly chastised. Having paid their "fines" to the tax collectors, the American sense of decency dictated that we get off their backs.

We need to tax energy, and to tax it heavily, to curb the profligacy that has become integral to our way of life. But we need to tax it where it will discourage consumption. A windfall profits tax creates the illusion that the government has done something about the continuing energy problem. Eventually, we'll realize that in our desire to punish the oil companies we only succeeded in punishing ourselves.

During the windfall tax debate the buzz phrase "obscene oil profits" was frequently used by journalists. This description of oil profits raises interesting questions. When do profits become obscene? We're supposed to believe in free enterprise. And the definition of free enterprise we're taught during our school days is that it's a system "motivated by profit, guided by price, and regulated by competition." So, not all profits can be obscene.

As it turns out, conventional economists have an answer to the rhetorical question raised above, although they prefer the term "excess" to "obscene." A company should earn enough profit, they say, to attract the investment funds it needs for the expansion of plant and equipment—if expansion is called for—as well as for the replacement of worn-out plant and equipment. Anything above this, they assert, represents "excess profits," or "economic rent." In theory, all of the excess could be taxed without reducing entrepreneurial initiative.

As is true of so much of conventional economic theory, however, this answer is too facile to be useful. There is no simple way to decide how much the oil companies need to spend on exploration (which is an important part of their "expansion" investment). Also, few corporations rely on outside capital for either expansion or replacement spending. They retain as much of their earnings as they think they will need. The rest is paid as dividends to stockholders. Thus, while the theory is precise, it is useless as a guide to policy. Any effort by Congress to determine how much of an oil company's profits are excess would be purely arbitrary.

The notion of "obscene" oil profits is the latest in a long line of scapegoats cooked up by well-meaning but misguided social critics. Financial writers pointed out that during one quarter of 1978, profit reports showed Texaco up 158 percent, Sohio 191 percent, Conoco 134 percent, Mobil 131 percent, and Gulf 97 percent. They didn't give equal billing to a sample of distillers who reported an increase of 162 percent. Evidently, the demand for booze is going up faster than the demand for gasoline.

Other manufacturers whose profits that quarter could have been mentioned included: farm equipment, up 242 percent; nonferrous metals mining, up 245 percent; and pulp and paper products, up 115 percent. Are those profits also "obscene"? They were not referred to as such. But all of those industries were doing better than the oil companies. Two of them reported increases much larger than the most profitable oil company.

All of these percentage changes raise another interesting question: How representative are any single quarter's profits? If all of the above industries—including oil—reported such prodigious profit increases every year, no one could reasonably argue against an "excess" profits tax, no matter how arbitrary it might be. But even in the oil industry, which has been raising consumer prices more or less steadily since

1973, profits vary widely from year to year. Anthony Parisi, an energy expert who wrote for the *New York Times*, has pointed out that for the five years through 1978, the oil industry's rate of return was no higher than that of all industry.

One needn't be a logician to recognize why oil profits are singled out for criticism. Everyone is affected in one way or another by the rising cost of energy. The impacts are particularly severe at the low end of the income scale and for those with fixed incomes. If the price of liquor becomes too high, one might have to give up drinking. And we don't feel the effects of high prices for farm equipment, nonferrous metals, or paper products as soon—or as directly—as the rising prices of gasoline and heating oil. We might suspect that there are many demons at work. But the ones that can be seen—and possibly exorcised—are those responsible for high oil prices.

Attacking profits is working on the wrong end of the problem. U.S. oil consumption has to be curtailed even more than it has been by rising prices. The most sensible way to do this would be by heavy taxes on oil products, especially gasoline. This would raise revenue directly, and quickly, to provide subsidies to those unable to pay their energy bills. High consumer taxes, coupled with a system of rationing using freely negotiable coupons, is the only approach that will bring the long-range energy situation under some semblance of control.

Rationing: Myths and Reality

There are three ways to deal with a shortage of any commodity deemed a "necessity": (1) let the free market handle it, (2) use a system of allocation, or (3) go all the way to rationing.

Free market supporters believe that rising prices will stimulate enough new production to cause an oversupply, and the oversupply in turn will result in declining prices. They assume, of course, an unlimited supply of the basic resource.

Only those who keep their heads perpetually buried in sand still believe in unlimited oil supplies. So we have had half-hearted attempts at allocation programs. The California "odd-even" system allowed half the car owners in the state to compete for each day's available supply of gasoline. This is a wasteful method of distributing available supplies. Cars lined up at filling stations burn gasoline, pollute the air, and go nowhere while waiting.

Allocation schemes can be as inequitable as the free market solution. Any allocation scheme has to have a base period. This is usually the same month of the prior year. This year's allocation is then some percentage of the base year. Gasoline consumption is seasonal, so this might appear to be a rational basis for making allocations. But the distribution of oil, and its derivatives, is a complex process. It goes from producer to storage tanks, to refineries, then to other storage tanks, to jobber-distributors, and finally to retail service stations.

Where large storage tanks are involved, the flow isn't necessarily even over time. If a wholesale distributor filled his tanks on August 1 of last year, for example, he might have had enough to carry him until the first of October. But say this year his tanks run dry in mid-September. The record shows he bought no gasoline in September last year. So he's entitled to none this year.

Multiply this hypothetical case by the hundreds of thousands of links between producers of crude oil and final consumers, and you'll see that it's virtually impossible to devise an allocation procedure that will not be wasteful, inequitable, and ineffective.

Several polls conducted during the late 1970s showed that the American public was ready for rationing. Even a few economists had suggested that it should be tried. One objection to rationing, however, is that a huge bureaucracy would be needed to administer the program. We now have a bureaucratic network that extends from Washington to the county level. A rationing program could be administered through the present loosely interdependent system. Some people might have to work harder than they now do, but huge new staffs wouldn't be needed.

A second objection is that rationing will inevitably lead to a "black market." Not if it is conducted on an "open-market" basis. This would be not only an efficient but also an equitable rationing system. Under an open-market system every household (not every individual or every car) would be entitled to a basic ration. This would be determined by dividing the total number of gallons available for sale by the number of households in the country. There would have to be additional allocations to farmers and other producers of essential commodities and services. Those could be handled on a case-by-case method.

All ration coupons would be freely negotiable. Members of households without cars would, of course, sell their coupons. Others could sell all or part of their ration. Only the specified number of gallons would be sold at fixed prices throughout the country. Those prices would, of course, take into account regional differences in delivery costs.

There would be no need for a black market if ration coupons were freely available on the open market. And members of households without cars are just as entitled to gasoline as those with one or more cars. Furthermore, using the household as the rationing unit would encourage more careful planning of automobile usage and fewer single-person trips. There would be bugs to work out. But the problems of a workable rationing system would be miniscule compared to those the nation would face if OPEC imposed another embargo as the result of some unexpected political or military crisis. The nation came close to panic during the short embargo of 1974. We're even less prepared now than we were then to cope with a sudden interruption to oil supply.

Anthony Downs, a Senior Fellow at the Brookings Institution, has said that "all non-market rationing systems are inherently *unfair*" (*Washington Post*, August 9, 1979, italics in the original). He specifically mentioned the scheme of allocating ration coupons to households and allowing householders to sell "excess" coupons in "white markets." The point Downs seems to have missed is that this method isn't a non-market method of rationing. It is a *market* rationing system. The "true" retail price of gasoline would be the price paid at the pump plus the price paid for the coupon. If an individual paid nothing for a coupon—if one used only the basic ration—the retail price would be the pump price. But if one bought coupons on the open market, the price of gasoline would be the pump price plus the price of the coupon. This could be any amount buyers of coupons were willing to pay.

Economists who believe in the efficacy of the free market appear to confuse fairness with the impersonality of the market mechanism. Adam Smith's "invisible hand" is impersonal enough. But it certainly doesn't guarantee that people will be treated fairly by the economic system. If wealth and income were equally distributed, we could agree that the free market would produce fair decisions. But with the wide disparities in income and wealth that exist—and with a very imperfectly functioning "free" market—it only confuses the issue to talk about the distribution of anything using fairness as the basic criterion.

The "Gas Guzzle" Myth

The *Wall Street Journal* tries to keep economists honest, particularly those who don't agree with the editors' conservative convictions. So it was with relish that the *Journal* editors attacked the "Gas Guzzle Myth" in their December 28, 1979 issue.

What is this myth? It's that the demand for gasoline is extremely inelastic. This is a perverse theory, they said, which "somehow popped up" to guide the miscalculations of politicians when they were "laying the groundwork for the energy mess" in the early 1970s. The *Journal* editors appear to know even less about economic history, however, than they do about economic theory. The idea that the U.S. demand for gasoline is relatively inelastic is an old one. It goes back much farther than the early 1970s. And in spite of the great discovery, reported in the late-December editorial, the demand for gasoline is still *relatively* inelastic.

What does all this mean? Where did the editors get the idea that gas guzzling in the United States is a myth? To answer the second question first, they gave Alan Greenspan (President Nixon's chief economic adviser) credit for exploding the myth. He appeared to be willing to accept their editorial accolade.

The elasticity of demand is a technical notion. It's hedged about with restrictive assumptions which economists rarely make clear in popular discussions. It can be calculated using formulas of varying degrees of complexity, but the basic formula is very simple:

$$\text{Price elasticity} = \frac{\text{Percentage change in quantity taken}}{\text{Percentage change in price}}.$$

Since there are percentage changes in both the numerator and denominator, this is a *relative* measure, a fact which seems to have eluded the *Journal* editors.

The idea is grasped easily by working out a few examples. Say the price of something goes up 10 percent (to keep the arithmetic easy), and the quantity purchased drops 20 percent. In this case price elasticity is 2. Economists would say that the demand for this product is relatively elastic. It means that consumers are very responsive to price changes.

But assume the opposite. Say the price of something goes up 50 percent, while the quantity purchased drops only 10 percent. Price elasticity in this case is 0.2, and economists say the demand for this product is relatively inelastic. The dividing line between relative elasticity and relative inelasticity is 1, which is called "unit elasticity." So the demand for any product is relatively inelastic as long as the elasticity coefficient is less than 1.

Greenspan found that during the prior year gasoline prices had risen by more than one-third in real terms; that is, gasoline prices increased one-third more than the average price level. But domestic demand, according to Greenspan, fell almost 10 percent. "That implies," the editors said, "an elasticity of close to 0.3, considerably higher than the most generous of previous estimates which have usually been no more than 0.2." This, they asserted magisterially, shows that "gasoline demand was found to be even more elastic than [Greenspan] had expected." They go on to quote Greenspan: "This may well be the most important statistic that has emerged from the Iranian crisis' aftermath."

This finding doesn't mean at all what the *Journal* editors say it means. First, the decline in gasoline consumption was closer to 7 than to 10 percent, although that difference is of no great significance to the present discussion. But even using Greenspan's figures, what it means is that the demand for gasoline is *less inelastic* than was previously believed. That isn't just a semantic distinction. There is a world of difference between the demand for something being more elastic and less inelastic. One is on the north side of unit elasticity, the other on the south.

If the U.S. demand for gasoline were elastic, rising prices would cause a sharp decline in consumption. The fact that gasoline demand is relatively inelastic is the reason that gradually rising prices have cut demand only slightly. Whether the measure of elasticity is 0.2 or 0.3 is not all that significant.

"We're glad," the *Journal* editors concluded, "that Mr. Greenspan has finally put the no-elasticity theory to rest." Their faith is touching, but their understanding of the problem was clearly faulty. The elasticity of demand for gasoline is of more than academic interest—it has important policy implications. If it were in fact relatively elastic, the market would sooner or later eliminate any shortage, real or contrived. But if the demand is relatively inelastic—as even Greenspan's calculations show—there is only one way to effectively curb our insatiable appetite for gasoline. That is by some method of rationing. The free-market method discussed above is consistent with conservative principles. Since they oppose rationing of any sort, however, even the free market aspect of this proposal is not likely to appeal to them.

Money Markets and Energy Markets

One of the causes of inflation is the rising price of imported oil. But since the dollars used to buy oil ultimately return to pay for American goods and services, inflation affects OPEC dollars just as it does domestic dollars. OPEC officials have responded by raising oil prices again, adding to the forces of inflation. So it has gone, in a seemingly endless spiral—or at least one that will last until oil becomes so costly we'll have to cut down on its use.

Not all of OPEC's customers are affected in the same way. The impact of rising oil prices in a particular country depends on the "price" of the dollar in that country's currency. Now that the world is back on a system of "floating" exchange rates, dollars are bought and sold at different prices in different countries. Each country has its own money market. Changes in the price of dollars between 1970 and 1979 in five other currencies are given in Table 1.

Table 1
Number of Units of Foreign Currency per Dollar

	1970	*1979*
Japan (yen)	336.00	197.90
West Germany (mark)	3.65	1.85
France (franc)	5.53	4.24
Italy (lira)	627.16	883.33
Spain (peseta)	70.00	69.10

Source: Roy W. Jastram, *Wall Street Journal* (January 16, 1979).

Even the Spanish peseta, not ordinarily regarded as one of the world's key currencies, held up better than the dollar during this period. The best bargain, among the countries shown, was the Italian lira. In 1970, one could get only 627 lira per dollar; in 1979 that figure was up to 883.

Japan and West Germany are major trading partners. American goods and services had become less expensive in these two countries, while the goods and services we bought from them cost more. One of the important services exchanged is travel. A trip to the U.S. became a bargain for the Japanese and West Germans, but it was increasingly expensive for Americans to go to those countries.

Money markets operate like the markets described in economics textbooks. Exchange rates are determined by demand and supply. If the supply of dollars in world markets increases faster than the demand for them in a particular country, the price of the dollar will drop in relation to the currency of that country. Japan provides the best illustration of this situation.

For years after World War II international bankers worried about a dollar "shortage." The demand for American goods was so strong that the dollar was bid up in terms of other currencies. Partly because of huge military and foreign aid expenditures—which were not offset by a return flow of goods and services from the recipient countries—world money markets accumulated "surplus" dollars. During the 1970s the dollar became worth progressively less in a number of major money markets.

That isn't the whole story, however. Any country whose currency has gained at the expense of the dollar has earned an extra bonus if it also buys OPEC oil. The way this works was described by Roy W. Jastram in the article from which the exchange ratios in Table 1 were taken.

World oil prices are quoted in terms of a "marker" oil—Saudi Arabian light crude—and expressed in dollars. The 400 percent price increase in 1974 hit all international buyers equally. Whatever the exchange rate at the time, each country had to acquire more dollars to pay for oil. But during the 1970s, the franc, the mark, and especially the yen gained on the dollar in international monetary exchange. That meant, effectively, that while the price of oil continued to rise in the U.S., it dropped in France, West Germany, and Japan. Jastram estimated that between 1976 and November 1978 the price of a barrel of oil delivered in the U.S. went up 10.4 percent. During the same period, it dropped 4 percent in France, 12.3 percent in West Germany, and a whopping 28.4 percent in Japan.

The price of energy is an important component of manufacturing costs, so the spread in oil prices between the U.S. and some of its more active trading partners had a double-barreled effect. It gave them an additional competitive advantage in world markets which, in turn, increased the demand for their currencies. As a result, the price of dollars, in terms of francs, marks, and yen, continued to drop.

There was a slight improvement in early 1981 as world oil prices stabilized while the general price level continued to rise. The position of the dollar improved slightly, but it came nowhere close to the 1970 relationships given in Table 1.

The position of the dollar would be further strengthened if the U.S. would sharply curtail imports of OPEC oil. That would reduce the number of dollars in world money markets and improve the dollar's position in international exchange. In the politically conservative climate of the early 1980s, no one appeared willing to risk the wrath of voters by taking the unpopular steps that would be required to limit oil—or, more specifically, gasoline—consumption. The likelihood is that we'll limp along, complaining every step of the way, until market forces slowly but inexorably accomplish the same result.

The Energy Crisis and Long-Range Energy Policy

The most vocal critics of policies emphasizing energy conservation are those who believe there is no problem. The United States doesn't have a "true" oil shortage, they say. We've been victimized by the oil companies. Most of those critics haven't the vaguest idea what the actual energy supply situation is. If they were told, they wouldn't believe it, and they find support for their position in the writings of "eminent" economists. (An "eminent" economist, incidentally, is one who agrees with your preconceptions. Those who don't are either "merely theorists" or "poorly informed.")

The fact is, conventional economists—eminent or otherwise—pay little attention to supply problems. Traditional economics emphasizes demand. The answer to supply problems, say conventional economists, is to let rising prices encourage production. This, strangely, is also the prescription of the "new" supply-side economists who came to prominence in the early 1980s. The prescription works under some circumstances. An example is the response of natural gas production when prices were allowed to rise. But certain conditions have to exist before this prescription will work. First, and most important, an adequate reserve supply must exist before higher prices will encourage sellers to increase their offerings of any product. The natural gas was available so there was no shortage. But how long will this situation last?

Resource economists, unlike their more numerous and better-known brethren, concentrate on supply. There is widespread agreement among them that the world's store of natural gas is being depleted rapidly. Even the more optimistic projections show little natural gas—at a price anyone would be willing to pay—by the turn of the century.

If we can't rely on oil, and if we'll soon be out of gas, what next? The two energy sources now available in relative abundance are coal and nuclear power. Coal can be converted to gas and oil. The cost of conversion is high, but thanks to OPEC it is now feasible to augment our oil supply by coal conversion.

Environmentalists oppose the expansion of coal and nuclear energy because both are heavy polluters. Every nuclear "incident," such as that at Three Mile Island, strengthens the environmentalists' position. Whatever else it might accomplish, the endless debate over the increased use of coal and nuclear energy will slow the development of these two sources. Surface-mined coal capacity can be expanded rapidly, although environmental constraints must again be kept in mind. The lead-time for constructing nuclear facilities continues to increase. It used to be five years. Now some engineers say it's nine. Every proposed new plant has to overcome opposition before construction can start.

The only alternative that has the blessing of virtually everyone is solar energy. But as the early philosophers used to say, it's an *ignis fatuus*—an illusion—to believe that solar energy will ever provide more than a fraction of the nation's energy needs. Still, solar energy supporters pressure for more research money. Meanwhile, support for coal gasification and coal liquefaction—both of which are technologically and economically feasible—is delayed by interminable hearings and demands for further study.

So the debate goes on. The number of publications on the energy issue increases exponentially. Instead of converging toward a consensus, however, the growing discussion seems to harden already crystallized positions. The sun worshipers become more adamant. The "anti-nukes" gain strength. The coal lobby is attacked by environmentalists. And almost everyone, it seems, regards measures that would insure effective conservation—probably the only approach that could work in the short-run—with skepticism.

Somehow this impasse has to be broken or the country is headed for a genuine crisis. It could come without warning from a number of directions. Whatever form it takes, we won't be ready. It could be avoided, but only if the hard-shell convictions of single-issue groups can be cracked. This might mean somewhat more detritus in the air and more scum in the water than most of us would like. It would mean accepting reasonable risks in the nuclear area since the only place there is no risk at all is in the cemetery. Most of all—and most difficult—it would require behavioral changes to force conservation. And these changes, probably, could only be brought about by such unpopular measures as substantially higher taxes on consumers, rationing, or a combination of the two.

It's ironic that each of the firmly held energy convictions is defensible when viewed in isolation. It's only when they come together that they form an impenetrable barrier to a workable long-range energy policy.

The oil glut of the 1980s, coupled with President Reagan's determination to reduce the scope of the federal establishment, effectively halted efforts to reach agreement on a long-range energy policy. In the words of Charles Ebinger, of the Georgetown Center for Strategic and International Studies: "President Reagan's failure to take the energy crisis seriously is a prescription for disaster later in the decade" (*Wall Street Journal*, February 25, 1982, p. 21).

His views were shared by Richard Kessler, who worked with Ebinger on a two-year energy-policy study. The prevailing view in the Reagan administration, Kessler said, was that oil prices were going to remain low. The decision to dismantle the Department of Energy and to cut back on conservation and research were, Kessler stated, "a program for disaster."

Americans have short memories, and the euphoria engendered by the decline of gasoline prices was reinforced by a sharp drop in the rate of inflation, itself a consequence of declining energy prices. Predictably, interest in the discussion of energy matters dropped off sharply, if only for the moment. A number of ideas advanced by writers who take a longer view are discussed in the following chapter.

Chapter 4

ENERGY FUTURE: SOLAR AND OTHER TECHNOLOGICAL PANACEAS

The Oil Company Conspiracy: A Non-Conventional View

A national protest against rising energy prices was organized in October 1979. It was a predictable failure. But several older persons—genuinely worried about the threat of a severe winter—were interviewed by TV reporters. Their messages came through loud and clear. They would face a series of "winters of discontent" unless something could be done to protect low-income households from rising fuel oil prices.

It is probably no coincidence that several long articles attacking the oil companies appeared a week before the protests. Robert Sherrill, writing in the October 14 *New York Times Magazine*, assailed the oil companies with the intensity of a Don Quixote. He presented a fifty year history of the "phony emergencies . . . engineered by" the American petroleum industry. Clearly, he regards the oil companies as malevolent oppressors.

Most of Sherrill's facts are correct, but they're highly selective. Someone with a bias in the opposite direction could write an account of the petroleum industry's past contributions to economic growth and rising real income in the U.S. The facts in such an account would be equally unassailable. They would also be incomplete.

Criticizing a champion of the oppressed can be tricky. Readers who divide all opinions into two categories—those for and those against an issue—might conclude that one who criticizes Sherrill must support the oil companies. Nothing, however, could be further from the truth. I have long maintained that the oil companies have "conspired" with government to influence petroleum prices, and indirectly, all other fossil fuel prices. But contrary to popular belief, the purpose of the "conspiracy" has been to keep oil prices low—not to raise them—in order to stimulate massive increases in consumption. This "conspiracy," incidentally, was until recent years completely successful. What Sherrill and those who share his views fail to point out is that until 1969 oil prices in the U.S. fell steadily relative to other prices.

How did the "conspiracy" work? Quite simply. The oil companies convinced legislators that oil should be taxed lightly. If the U.S. had taxed oil at the rates imposed by Western European governments, the economic history of the past quarter-century would have been different. The wasteful habits engendered by cheap oil would not have developed. There would have been fewer "gas guzzlers." Houses would have been properly insulated.

Artificially low oil prices—relative to world prices—encouraged American industry to adopt wasteful production methods. Higher oil prices would have stimulated the continued expansion of coal. An effective system of mass transportation would have been in place long ago. Without our insatiable appetite for imported oil, the international cartel might have remained nothing more than a gleam in the eye of the late Juan Pablo Perez Alfonso, the Venezuelan architect of OPEC.

In short, the problem isn't that U.S. energy prices have become too high; it's that they were artificially depressed before 1973. No one will ever know how much energy we squandered during the era of cheap oil. But if high taxes had forced industry and households to strive for a high level of "energy efficiency"—as OPEC's efforts are doing today—we might have stretched the world's oil supply for another half century.

What do Sherrill and those of like mind want the government to do? They want it to get into the oil and gas business. They're not proposing socialization of the industry. They suggest that government enterprises compete with private firms. Then the government wouldn't have to rely on the industry for data on costs, inventories, and other critical information. It could compile its own.

As Sherrill points out, this is an ancient idea. Fortunately, it generates as little enthusiasm today as when it was first presented. We didn't need such competition before 1973. The oil industry and government kept prices below competitive levels. And the idea makes no sense at all today. The age of cheap energy is gone for good. From here on, worldwide demand will exceed worldwide supply. That means continued price increases.

Is the government helpless in this situation? Not at all. It's still not too late to impose a high tax on oil and gasoline. Consumers and industry are beginning to be serious about energy conservation. Doubling the price of gasoline and oil by taxation would lead to additional conservation. And it would provide the revenue needed to subsidize low-income and fixed-income households. That is the only way helpless and needy members of our society can be protected from rising energy prices.

It's doubtful that our timorous politicians will impose such taxes, certainly not as long as they are under the influence of "Reaganomics," so we might be headed for real trouble. That trouble won't be avoided by deregulation, by assailing the oil companies, or by flogging other dead horses that have nothing to do with a practical solution.

Gasoline Prices and Gasoline Taxes

U.S. residents burn roughly one-third of the world's output of gasoline. We do this because—in spite of recent price increases—gasoline is cheaper here than in most other countries which rely on imports for a large part of total usage. Table 2 tells the story starkly. It shows how U.S. gasoline prices compared with those of selected countries in late 1979. It's doubtful that the relationships have changed significantly since then.

The three West European countries paid more in gasoline taxes than the average retail price of a gallon of gas in the United States. It's easy to understand their chagrin at our failure to curb consumption

Table 2

Gasoline Prices and Taxes
In Five Western Countries—1979

	Price per U.S. Gallon	Tax Amount	Percent of Price
U.S.	$1.01	.14	14%
Great Britain	$1.99	.88	44
West Germany	$2.25	$1.16	52
Italy	$2.48	$1.62	65
France	$2.71	$1.69	62

Source: *New York Times*, November 25, 1979.

more effectively. Without our voracious appetite for gasoline, world oil prices couldn't have risen as fast as they have.

Congressman John Anderson, who ran as an independent candidate for president in 1980, introduced a bill which would have raised the tax on gasoline to 50 cents a gallon. Many editorial writers, faithfully reflecting their readers' belief in the sanctity of unrestrained driving, expressed outrage. But at $1.50 per gallon, taxes would still account for only 33 percent of the retail price. The more timorous supporters of Anderson's bill wanted even this modest hike in the gas tax to be made in small increments so the effects could be "absorbed" by consumers. Even that modest proposal fell by the wayside.

Allowing a tax to creep up slowly—perhaps just enough to keep pace with inflation—wouldn't discourage consumption. It would bring in more revenue, but not enough to support the development of alternative energy sources—or to subsidize the low-income groups who are already in trouble.

How high a tax would it take to discourage the present profligate consumption of gasoline? J. K. Galbraith once suggested $5 per gallon. A $5 tax would force conservation all right; it would also create chaos throughout the economy. The answer to the question raised above depends on the elasticity of demand for gasoline discussed earlier. This, as noted, has been relatively inelastic, but that's because price increases have been spread over a fairly long period. What would happen, however, if the price jumped to the neighborhood of $2.50 a gallon by the imposition of a $1 per gallon tax? With that large a jump, daily purchases might drop.

We've had enough experience to learn that slowly rising gasoline prices alter consumption habits only marginally. But it's likely that at $2.50 per gallon there would be more serious conservation efforts. At that price the demand for gasoline could be in the elastic range.

Even at higher prices market forces alone should not be allowed to dictate the distribution of gasoline. Along with a major tax hike, a lid should be put on gasoline consumption by rationing. As discussed earlier, each household (not each vehicle) would be given a quota, and ration coupons would be freely negotiable. That would be a democratic form of rationing which would rely as much as possible on the free market.

What are the prospects for a program which would: (a) encourage immediate conservation efforts, (b) enhance the prospects of a public transportation system, (c) encourage the search for alternative energy sources, and (d) spread the burden of conservation equitably over the population? They're not good.

Too many politicians are fearful of interfering with the love affair between Americans and their automobiles. Too many technological optimists continue to promise a gullible public that somewhere over the horizon there's an easy answer to the energy problem. And the laid-back public refuses to get aroused. There's gasoline enough today, so let's enjoy it! After all, only a few pessimistic cranks keep harping that maybe there won't be enough to go around tomorrow.

Energy Future: The Harvard Connection

Energy Future, the report of a special energy project conducted at the Harvard Business School, and published by Random House in 1979, enjoyed an unusual distinction among scholarly books. It made the best-seller list. It would be comforting to say that it shed new light on the nation's energy problem, and that it provided useful suggestions for a long-range national energy policy. Unfortunately, it did neither.

There's a lot in the book that any reasonable student of the energy situation can agree with. It's free of bilious diatribes against OPEC, although it gives too much weight to the effects of "political accidents" in the Mideast as causes of oil price increases. The Harvard report will delight the solar lobby. Its authors believe the sun can directly provide 20 percent of the country's energy needs by the turn of the century. They follow the solar lobby line of urging that windfall profits from oil be used to finance solar research. There's no suggestion of using part of the receipts as a rebate to the poor.

They don't see much of a future for coal. This source of energy, the authors assert, might have long-term potential but can't be very helpful in the near-term. That's a novel idea. Most energy analysts believe that unless the U.S. cuts back sharply on energy consumption, coal will have to provide an increasing share of the nation's energy between now and the end of the century.

The authors' basic recommendation agrees with that of a number of other recent energy studies. Conservation, they tell us, is the only immediate answer to the energy crisis. A barrel of oil saved is far cheaper than any other alternative. They hasten to disassociate themselves, however, from those who believe that conservation implies slower economic growth. Here they become mildly emotional about the "anti-growth crusade led by . . . granola-chomping children of the affluent."

It's seriously misleading to suggest that anyone who questions the desirability or feasibility of continued economic growth is a hippie, or one of the latter-day derivatives of that diminishing species. There is a growing body of very respectable scientific thought concerned with the physical and technological limits to growth.

The Harvard team is on shaky statistical ground when it asserts that the United States could have enjoyed its present standard of living while consuming 40 percent less energy than it did. There's no question that we're the most profligate energy consumers in the world, and there's no question that we could have achieved a high level of real per capita income while consuming less energy. But the estimate that we've wasted 40 percent of the energy consumed is on the high side.

The most serious weakness of the Harvard study is the implication that the United States can emerge from the energy crisis without fundamental changes in life style. Its authors believe that if the auto industry shifted its emphasis from styling to a search for energy efficiency it could produce cars that would get 50 miles per gallon. They seem to accept the automobile as integral to the American way of life. They're not much impressed by proposals for auto pooling or mass transportation because they lack "the convenience desired by the American public." That kind of statement drives Europeans up the wall. They regard the American attitude toward the private auto as a "convenience" with understandable annoyance. "What makes you think," they ask, "that you're entitled to five times as much energy per person as the rest of the world?" There's no rational answer to that question.

The Harvard study notwithstanding, U.S. dependence on the convenience of the private automobile won't last indefinitely. In fact, it might not last long. Articles have appeared in journals of opinion dealing with the transitory nature of the auto age. Some scholars are beginning to consider how the end of private transportation as we know it today might affect the size and structure of cities, the location of industry, and other matters that have been so drastically influenced by the ubiquitous American automobile. Not everyone is as sure as the authors of *Energy Future* appear to be that the "desire for convenience" will perpetuate the age of the private automobile.

Will *Energy Future*, on balance, help or hinder the search for a "solution" to the nation's energy problems? Since the study came from one of the more distinguished graduate schools of business in the country, it received a respectful hearing in Washington. It was quoted by several environmentalists on TV talk shows. Unfortunately, it's a very conventional book that adds nothing new to the continuing energy debate.

Its conclusions are what one would expect from a business school faculty. Rely on the marketplace as much as possible. Forget warnings that we'll all have to make sacrifices. They don't quite say it, but the authors strongly hint that there is such a thing as a free lunch. Increased efficiency is their substitute for the conventional trade-off of economic analysis. Efficiency, in the home and in auto factories, will get us off the energy hook. We've heard this line so often it has become banal. The Harvard report might not hinder the search for an effective energy policy; it surely won't help it.

Close on the heels of *Energy Future* came another optimistic energy assessment with a Harvard connection. That report, published by the independent Committee for Economic Development, was written by Thomas Schelling, Littauer Professor of Political Economy at Harvard, and a panel of business and educational leaders. A summary in *Harvard Magazine* (September–October 1979, p. 15) makes it clear that it's another addition to the growing stream of "not-to-worry" energy literature.

"The energy problem," the report states, "is not to keep the price of fuel from rising. It is to meet the rising economic cost of fuel with policies that minimize the burdens, allocate them equitably, avoid disruptions to the economy, and keep the costs from rising more than necessary." This is a superb statement of the problem. A majority of economists—regardless of persuasion—would agree with this succinct statement of the problem. But the report's conclusion is something else.

"Decently managed," Schelling and his associates say, "the energy component of our economy need not be expected to interfere seriously with employment and continual economic growth and it need not entail costs of a magnitude to deserve much attention from economic historians in the future." How they reached that conclusion isn't stated in the *Harvard Magazine* summary. It's another example of the energy optimism being peddled by persons of the highest scholarly repute. But it flies in the face of logic as well as the evidence of declining growth rates in all of the world's larger, industrialized nations.

How Long Can Growth Go On?

The idea that further increases in energy prices won't interfere with employment and continuous economic growth is sheer nonsense.

Conventional economists assume that the total supply of energy is unlimited. As one kind is used up, we'll shift to a substitute. As all present sources of energy are used up, new sources will appear. Economic growth, they imply, can go on forever. Part of the problem is that conventional economic thought has become inbred. Conventional economists read each others' writings, and draw comfort from their mutual support.

It's a pity more of them aren't familiar with the work of Albert A. Bartlett, a Harvard-trained physicist at the University of Colorado. He is the author of a widely known article on the "Forgotten Fundamentals of the Energy Crisis," and frequently speaks to student groups. His presentations, documented by a set of slides, evoke lively ovations. This is remarkable not only because students are rarely demonstrative after a lengthly, scholarly presentation, but also because Bartlett provides convincing evidence of the physical impossibility of continual economic growth in a finite environment. And the world—despite the assumptions of conventional economists—is a very finite environment. Using simple numerical examples, Bartlett explains the mathematical consequences of steady growth even when annual growth rates are small and declining.

Bartlett's message is anything but cheerful. Still, students respond enthusiastically. They demonstrate that they're far more interested in tightly reasoned projections than optimistic pap based on wishful thinking. The public at large might respond equally well if officials gave the same kind of honest assessment of the nation's future.

We've become victims of what Bartlett calls the "growth culture." We're led to believe that unless each generation consumes more than the generation before we aren't making progress. And progress has become the leitmotif of the American way of life. Bartlett shows that we can't continue to consume energy at anything close to the rate of the past two decades. During the 1970s alone, the U.S. consumed as much energy as it had throughout its entire past history. Anyone with a modicum of sense must realize that such accelerated growth can't continue. (More will be said about Bartlett's work in Chapter 5.)

The view that we can have continued economic growth without increased energy consumption assumes that we'll become more "energy efficient"—the economists' fancy term for conservation. Higher prices will force less energy use per person. Few question this. But the assumption that industry can squeeze enough waste out of its processes to turn out an ever-expanding volume of goods with declining energy inputs is far more doubtful. Even if it could, how long could this process go on?

A handful of economists—including such luminaries as Georgescu-Roegen, Robert Heilbroner, and the late E. F. Schumacher—have warned that mere survival will call for drastic changes in the way we live and work. Their arguments—unlike the thinking of conventional economists—aren't based on vague hopes about any "technical fixes" or other forms of wishful thinking. Like Bartlett's, they're based on hard facts.

The next and succeeding generations could adapt to life without a lot of the extravagances we now regard as essential. Do we need new clothing styles each year? Could we cut back on cosmetics? Couldn't we shift from "planned obsolescence" to maximizing the durability of goods? No reasonable student of the energy problem suggests that we're on the verge of returning to the Stone Age. There's every reason to believe, however, that by the turn of the century the growth culture will have vanished, and the central role of scarcity in economics will have been reestablished. As Schelling points out, the most important goal will be to "minimize the burdens of rising energy costs, and to allocate them equitably."

The Solar Solution

Supporters of a massive solar energy research program apparently believe that with adequate funding scientists could find ways to let the sun provide all or nearly all of our energy needs. No one doubts the desirability of the objective. Solar energy is clean. Under ideal conditions it can directly heat and cool homes. By means of photovoltaic cells sunlight can be converted to electric energy for industrial use. So what's the problem? Why aren't we going all out for solar energy?

One obstacle is economic. Another is unreliability. What about economic arguments? Would it be feasible to close all nuclear plants—

and many coal-burning plants—with the sun making up the deficit? Unfortunately, it wouldn't. Those who argue that widespread use of solar collecting devices is economically feasible ignore fundamental scientific principles.

The problem is the basic economic principle that "there's no such thing as a free lunch." It requires capital—plant and equipment—to convert any kind of energy from its free state into "work." We need boilers to burn coal, gas, and oil; reactors to obtain heat from uranium; and collectors (plus storage devices) to put sunbeams to work. As energy is used, it is transformed into waste heat. This process, in scientific jargon, is called entropy, and the entropy law is as reliable and predictable as the law of gravity.

If we need capital to transform free energy into useful forms, why not invest only in solar collectors and storage devices? The problem is that all equipment used to capture solar energy is manufactured by the use of fossil fuels or nuclear energy. There is not—and because of the entropy process never can be—a solar energy system that would produce a surplus of energy. That is what would be required if a solar energy system were to be self-sustaining.

The sad fact is that solar energy can play only a relatively small role in a broader energy system. Everyone favors the use of as much solar energy as is physically and economically feasible. But in the foreseeable future it can't be more than a marginal supplement to fossil and nuclear fuels. This situation won't be changed by funding more solar research projects. Available funds would be far better spent on efforts to reduce consumption. To paraphrase former Deputy Secretary John F. O'Leary's perspicacious comment on the gasoline crisis: "There isn't a shortage of energy. There's only a surplus of wasteful energy users."

During the last congressional term of the Carter Administration, a 109-member Congressional Solar Coalition was formed. The Coalition's laudable goal was to have the sun directly provide one-fourth of the nation's electricity needs by the end of the century. Unfortunately, a laudable objective isn't always enough. More than a year earlier, the White House had asked the American Physical Society to study the potential of solar energy. The long-term prospects for solar energy are favorable, the physicists reported, but it might be as long as a half-century before the sun can supply as much as 10 percent of the nation's electricity. According to an article in the *New York Times*, the Physical Society's report was branded as "distorted" and "irresponsible" by solar enthusiasts. Like other single-issue groups, this one isn't tolerant of those who dissent from the views it holds dear.

No one questions the desirability of greater reliance on solar energy. But solar technology is still experimental. There is presently no large-scale solar system that can compete with even the most expensive of fossil fuels. Solar advocates argue that the unique advantage of solar cells is that they can be made small enough to fit on single housetops. They don't discuss, however, the relative efficiency—or self-sufficiency—of such small units.

The intensity of solar radiation at the earth's surface is very weak. This problem can be dealt with by building large terrestrial collectors or by designing collectors to operate in outer space. One drawback of both proposed systems is that they would require enormous investment in plant and equipment. All of the equipment would have to be made by using fossil fuels or nuclear energy.

Georgescu-Roegen has given detailed and rigorous technological assessments of solar energy in the *Atlantic Economic Journal* (December 1978) and the *Southern Economic Journal* (April 1979). He agrees that the widespread use of solar energy would be desirable if it were technically and economically feasible. All of the "recipes" for collecting solar energy, as Georgescu so aptly describes them, make use of physical matter and fossil energy. And while solar energy might be "inexhaustible," matter and fossil fuels aren't. We worry about energy because so much of the world's known supply of fossil fuels has been depleted. If we use the remainder at an even faster rate by diverting materials to a solar-energy "industry"—before carefully working out all of the consequences—we might end up worse, not better, off.

It isn't a question of all or nothing. Houses with solar panels are being built every day, and scientists are doing research on more effective ways to store solar energy. But some solar advocates want more now. A major investment in solar energy, they say, would reduce anti-pollution, health-care, and other costs in the future. The question, however, is: How much could we afford to spend today for a program that would provide most of its benefits in the distant future?

Solar enthusiasts ignore other problems. How, for instance, would huge investments in solar energy affect inflation? A realistic energy policy has to include all feasible alternatives and their consequences. Others are asking for more federal funds. At the same time, voters responded to rising prices by electing a President, and an apparently tractable Congress, dedicated to increased federal austerity and increased reliance on the private sector of the economy. The wisdom of a cabal of Solomons couldn't cope with these contradictory trends and demands.

The Good News About Energy

The Council on Environmental Quality—CEQ for short—reports directly to the President on the state of the nation's environmental health. But during the latter half of the Carter administration the CEQ also became involved in the tricky business of economic prognostication. The reason wasn't hard to deduce. Environmental legislation has been identified as one of the causes of declining economic growth. So, if the CEQ could provide evidence that the economic outlook is bright, maybe the voices that have demanded a reduction in environmental standards as a spur to economic growth would be stilled.

We have been told by a number of conventional economists that if the U.S. can just get its growth rate up again we can have the best of both worlds—rising real income and a cleaner environment. The CEQ's cheerful projections are a reprise of this argument. They were given in a brief document—only 55 pages—called *The Good News About Energy*. It was not a report on new research; instead, it summarized the cheerful parts of several energy studies of varying degrees of technical complexity. Unlike most governmental documents, which are quite drab in appearance, this one is colorful. Its bright yellow cover enhances the sharp red type of the title. One approaches the report with great expectations.

The centerpiece, and the source of the good news about energy, is an ancient idea presented in a sprightly new dress. It's called "energy productivity," and the good news is that it's going to increase greatly during the years ahead. The informed public is familiar with the term "productivity." Generally, however, productivity—or efficiency—is related to labor inputs. Here the news hasn't been good. Labor productivity has been declining. Among the important causes of reduced labor productivity have been health, safety, and environmental legislation. But if this decline could be offset, and new growth engendered by rising energy productivity, the economic outlook would indeed be a cheerful one.

Energy productivity has increased since 1969, the year fossil fuel prices started to spiral upwards. Most of the increase came after 1974, when world oil prices were quadrupled. The CEQ doesn't deal with such mundane facts, however. It talks instead about the energy situation in the year 2000. By then, the CEQ confidently asserts, the nation will have reaped the benefits of enormous increases in energy efficiency.

What is the basis for this optimistic forecast? Does the CEQ know something about future technology the rest of us don't? Not at all. The projection is based on several well-known studies of energy wastefulness in the U.S. in the past. It's no secret that we are the most prodigal energy consumers in the world. But if energy is dirt cheap and other inputs are expensive—as was the case in the U.S. until 1969—it makes economic sense to use as much energy as possible and as little of everything else. This generalization applies to agriculture and to most lines of manufacturing.

It follows, again from elementary economic analysis, that when energy prices increase faster than other prices, as they have since 1974, producers will adapt to the new situation by substituting less costly inputs and conserving energy. Expensive energy will be used as efficiently as possible. Scientists and engineers will be called on to develop new production techniques that use less energy per unit of output.

Some studies have hypothesized that if we had invested in the best technology available today twenty or thirty years ago, we could have produced as much as we did last year with 30 to 40 percent less energy. By simple extrapolation, the CEQ concluded that we can continue to produce more in the future with less and less energy. But there's a subtle fallacy in this argument. If we had installed today's best available technology twenty years ago, the plant and machinery would have been built with cheap energy. Everything built in the future will use expensive energy.

Efforts to improve energy productivity have been stepped up since 1974, and there will be further energy savings in the future. It's a misuse of arithmetic, however, to simply project what we "could have done" in the past into the future. The easiest way to increase energy efficiency is to eliminate waste. This is being done. But other increases in energy productivity will come harder. Once the most palpable causes of waste have been eliminated, further energy savings from waste elimination will be made in progressively smaller increments. Like everything else in the economic system, energy productivity will encounter the law of diminishing returns.

In fairness to the CEQ, they were not alone in making cheerful economic prognostications at that time. The Union of Concerned Scientists—who are adamantly opposed to nuclear energy and almost as strongly opposed to the increased use of coal—also claims that we can have economic growth, as well as a safe and clean environment, as the result of massive increases in energy productivity. Their economic reasoning is no more defensible than that of the CEQ.

Everyone—not only those who fall under the "single issue" rubric—should be interested in increased energy efficiency. Anytime anything becomes scarce—a condition marked by sharp price increases—conservation becomes important. But nothing is gained by creating exaggerated expectations about the long run. The only one of Keynes's many dicta unchallenged today is his off-the-cuff remark that "in the long run we'll all be dead."

Can Modern Physics Solve the Energy Problem?

The *New Yorker* is an exceptional magazine famed for the quality of its fiction and verse. It also publishes lucid scientific articles. One example is a three-part series by Jeremy Bernstein (concluded in the

December 17, 1979, issue) about the distinguished Cornell physicist Hans Albrecht Bethe (pronounced like the Greek letter Beta). Since 1974 Bethe, although nominally retired, has been trying to find solutions to the energy problem. No one can question his accomplishments as a physicist. He was given the 1967 Nobel Prize in Physics for discovering the specific nuclear reactions that produce energy in the sun and other stars. Like other geniuses, however, Bethe at times wanders into fields in which he has had no training and has no particular competence. His views on economics, for example, shouldn't be taken seriously.

The problem, as Bethe sees it—or as his views are interpreted by Bernstein—is to produce enough energy to insure that the American standard of living will continue to increase. He posits a growth of 3 percent a year in Gross National Product. Bethe considers this a meager growth rate or "a starvation diet." But at this rate the real GNP would almost double by the year 2000. He may consider this to be "meager," but even the perennial optimists doubt that there is much chance that the U.S. can maintain such a high growth rate during the next two decades. This is roughly the period they consider to be "the transition" discussed in Chapter 1. Even if that growth rate could be maintained until the year 2000, what then? Would GNP continue to double every twenty years?

On energy matters Bethe's views are more convincing, although here too he will encounter skepticism. Even if some new and exotic technology were now available as an alternative source of energy, Bethe points out, it couldn't help the nation before the year 2000. It takes about twenty years for a major technological development to be applied.

Bethe believes that because of this technological lag, the energy gap can only be closed in the next twenty years by the rapid expansion of coal and nuclear power. Within forty years, in his view, we will have to produce more than 2.5 billion tons of coal annually. His knowledge of the coal industry, however, is superficial. He implies that Eastern coalfields are nearly worked out, and that almost all of the coal produced in the next century will come from the West. It isn't economical now, however—and it will be less economical in the future—to ship Western coal East of the Mississippi. Also, Eastern coal reserves are far from depleted. There will be major increases in coal production both in the East and the West between now and the end of the century.

Bethe, surprisingly, has little to say about synthetic fuels. Well before the year 2000, however, we are likely to be producing oil and gas from coal and possibly from shale. The synthetic fuels won't be cheap, but they should be competitive with oil before the end of the 1980s.

Bethe knows the time will come when all the non-renewable sources of energy on the earth will be gone. But his response to this is highly Utopian. To harness renewable energy sources—the sun, the oceans, the trees, the wind, the streams—a cooperative global effort will be required. Bethe feels that such cooperation will be achieved. "The next century may turn out to be a good time to be alive—a more benign time." The real problem, as he sees it, is how to get from here to there.

Bethe supports the expansion of nuclear energy—including "breeder" reactors. He claims there are fairly simple ways to handle nuclear wastes. But if waste disposal were as simple—and as safe—as Bethe makes it seem, further objection to the expansion of nuclear power would be irrational.

Bernstein revives an old bromide about the "breeder" reactor—without quoting Bethe—which requires careful interpretation. It is that the breeder will "produce more fuel than it consumes." This is easily confused with the millennial notion that the breeder produces more *energy* than it consumes. If that were true, we'd have perpetual motion. Unfortunately, the Second Law of Thermodynamics proves the latter delightful thought to be pure nonsense.

This excellent series of articles about one of the century's more gifted scientists is essentially a special plea for more nuclear energy. It's as good a case as has been made for this point of view. Unfortunately, there's another side to the story. Anyone who reads Bernstein's articles should read what the opposition is writing as well.

Nuclear Fusion: The *Deus ex Machina*

Ancient Greek dramatists used a clever device to rescue characters from seemingly hopeless situations. When the plot placed characters in a dilemma with no logical solution, a deity would be swung onto the stage to rescue the mortal or mortals involved. Later dramaturgists named this device the *deus ex machina*—literally, "god from the machine." The term has become part of our language. It's used to describe any situation where an "outside" force is expected to solve a presently unsolvable problem. Another name for this approach to problem-solving is the "Good Fairy Principle."

The most popular *deus ex machina* invoked these days is nuclear fusion. Numerous articles—in newspapers as well as scientific journals—have discussed this arcane topic in recent years. Some journalistic accounts have suggested that fusion energy might be available as early as 1984. That is palpable nonsense. The most optimistic forecast by a reputable scientist suggests we might have fusion-based power by 2020, and that forecast assumes that certain engineering problems which have been intractable up to now will have been solved.

What is nuclear fusion? Why is it the great hope of technological optimists in the face of the disappointing record of nuclear fission? A quarter of a century ago John von Neumann, a great mathematician and a pioneer in the development of atomic energy, said: "A few decades hence energy may be free—just like the unmetered air, with coal and oil used mainly as raw materials for organic chemical synthesis . . . ."

What was to be the source of this "free" energy? Nuclear reactors. Such expectations were common in 1955. Now nuclear power producers have to cope with new fears and obstacles raised by accidents such as that at Three Mile Island. And nuclear energy costs considerably more than that produced by coal-burning power plants.

It's important to reexamine early expectations about the Utopian existence that was supposed to be waiting for us following the advent of atomic energy, and to compare those expectations with today's reality. Exactly the same things are now being claimed for a future in which there will be an "unlimited supply" of very cheap (if not entirely free) energy from nuclear fusion. Some writer fifty years hence will look at these statements with the same wonder that von Neumann's forecast evokes today.

The sun is a gigantic fusion reactor. To produce fusion energy, scientists and engineers have to replicate this reactor on a very small scale. But there are problems. The sun's temperature is close to 100 million degrees Celsius, and this self-sustaining ball of fire generates pressures greater than 20 million pounds per square inch. This cosmic reactor is held in place by gravitation, so there's no need for artificial "containment" of such heat and pressure.

Terrestrial engineers will have to develop a "container" to substitute for gravity. It can't be made of material. No natural or man-made substance can withstand that much heat and pressure. So the terrestrial sun will have to be held in place by something similar to the "force fields" familiar to science fiction and space movie aficionados.

The raw material for fusion energy is hydrogen—just as it is in the sun, which burns 164 million tons of it per second. The fact that hydrogen can be obtained from water—probably the most plentiful substance on earth—is what gives rise to the myth that fusion energy will be "cheap." But the best that scientists hope for, if and when a fusion reactor is perfected, is that it will break even in energy terms; that it will produce as much energy as it consumes. That means the equipment used to make fusion reactors, like every other machine the world has ever known, will have to be manufactured using fossil fuels—coal, oil, and natural gas.

What the Utopians—who promise a cornucopian world once we have fusion power—overlook is the tremendous cost of the capital equipment that will be required. And that equipment will cost much more—in real terms—in 2020 than it would today.

Anyone with the mildest interest in the future of humanity hopes scientists and engineers can produce controlled nuclear fusion. Let's not be misled, however, by the well-meaning but naive optimists who tell us fusion energy will usher in a new age of abundance. By the time scientists and engineers have developed a magnetic "bottle" to contain a miniature sun, there will be—by conservative estimates—8 billion to 9 billion persons to be fed, clothed, housed and entertained. It will take all the energy the world can muster—as well as ingenuity which political leaders have not yet displayed, to convert the earth to a peaceful economic "container" for this population. Working out the details of this container will be as difficult, and just as important, as designing the one needed to produce fusion energy.

Chapter 5

TRANSITION TO
A BRAVE NEW WORLD

The Transition

Perhaps no word has been more overworked when economic problems are being discussed than "transition." Literally, transition means passage from one position, stage, or state to another. One can see why the term is favored by writers and conference speakers. Those who invoke it are able to avoid confrontation with serious and intractable issues. Whatever the problem— unemployment, inflation, pollution, slow growth—they assure us it will be taken care of eventually; that is, after the transition.

Logically, the statement that the world is going through a transition is unassailable. Since time is irreversible (except in space-age movies), the world is constantly passing from one state to another. Everything we do involves transition because of the ineluctable passage of time. There is no guarantee, of course, that things will be better after some unspecified transitional period than they were before, although that is implicit in the views of technological optimists if the statement is not made explicitly.

The Club of Rome is a somewhat shadowy organization which describes itself as "an informal international group of 100 individuals." It is best-known for its sponsorship of a book called *The Limits to Growth* by Dennis and Donella Meadows, published in 1972. That book, which sold millions of copies, predicted a global catastrophe during the next century because of resource depletion, environmental degradation, and the Malthusian tendency for population growth to outrun food supplies. The book was attacked by scores of technological optimists because its authors failed to realize that all the problems it discussed are transitional. The critics will be dead, of course, before the predicted catastrophe is supposed to occur. So will the authors of *The Limits to Growth*. Neither the Utopians nor the catastrophists will be around to say "we told you so," in case either side should turn out to be right.

The world is in a constant state of flux; things are changing all the time. Scholars can mark off historical stages, however, such as the Middle Ages, the Age of Discovery, or other periods which historians have set in brackets to help describe how mankind got from there to here. It's doubtful, however, that even the most stubborn believer in historical stages would argue that those whose lives spanned more than one era knew they were going through a transition.

Transitions aren't like wars, love affairs, or other events that begin and end on specific dates. Anyone who has spent five or six decades on this remarkable planet has gone through several transitions. But like Moliere's character who went through life without realizing that he spoke prose, most of us weren't aware of it at the time.

A recent buzzword in the arcanum of transitionalists is "reindustrialization." Transitionalists who accept this notion believe that while things are tough now—and might even get worse in the years immediately ahead—a bright future can be guaranteed if present behavior patterns can be changed. The term "reindustrialization" appears to have been coined by Amitai Etzioni, then a professor of sociology at George Washington University. While the word is new, it describes an ancient and disarmingly simple notion.

The notion of reindustrialization is a response to an earlier idea, called the post-industrial society, which was developed by Harvard sociologist Daniel Bell. The essence of the post-industrial argument is that America should concentrate on high-technology activities—such as computers and the new information industry—and let developing countries produce the world's goods. This way, post-industrialists say, everyone will benefit. The basis for that conclusion is an ancient economic apothegm called the principle of comparative advantage.

But, countered Etzioni, if we listen to the post-industrial gurus, who will provide the goods needed for national defense? Also, aren't we already overly dependent on foreign sources of energy? The post-industrialists, Etzioni implies, aren't realistic. If we export industrial jobs, America will become increasingly vulnerable to military and economic assault. Instead of allowing the U.S. industrial establishment to continue to wind down—as it has been doing for more than a decade—we need to rebuild the industrial sector. One gathers that Etzioni, and those who agree with him, would like to see the United States again become the preeminent industrial nation of the world.

How would this be done? No major institutional changes would be required. Specific proposals for reindustrialization are quite conventional. What the country needs, the argument goes, is more saving and investment; obsolete machinery and equipment must be replaced; alternative sources of energy must be expanded, especially coal; invention and innovation must be stimulated.

For a decade, the reindustrialists believe, Americans would have to forego a rising standard of living. But this wouldn't be as bad as it sounds. Americans already have had a decade or more of little or no increase in the average standard of living. Sacrificing consumption today, however, will guarantee more consumption later. The anticipation of a future good life—something on the order of the 1960s, with its 2 percent annual real growth rate—would help sustain the population during the decade of sacrifice.

Etzioni's critique of the post-industrial hypothesis is sound. That hypothesis was based on the same simplifying assumptions that lie behind most futuristic pipedreams. But Etzioni's reindustrialization hypothesis is only slightly more realistic. Like other proposals to "get America moving again," it ignores resource constraints and assumes that the nation's economic problems can be solved by increasing the economic growth rate. Etzioni has only said what scores of conventional economists have been saying since the economy started to slow down in 1969. His contribution was to coin a catchy buzzword which some politicians attempted to exploit to the limit.

The reindustrialists evidently believe that America's problems are unique. They aren't. To some degree, all industrial nations—including Japan and West Germany—have experienced sharp declines in growth rates. It's true that the U.S. drop has been more pronounced than most, but the problems of mature industrialization are global, not national or local. They are the result of another ancient and apodictic economic principle, the law of diminishing returns.

With a fixed quantity of land, dwindling energy and natural resources, and a burgeoning global population, the rate of economic growth in the world's older industrial nations had to slow down. The members of OPEC have experienced accelerated growth, but that will continue only for a limited time. Meanwhile, Third World countries—which include three-fourths of the world's people—haven't grown at all. Some have slipped backward.

One need not agree with the assumptions of the reindustrialists to agree with their policy proposals. The U.S. should save and invest more; efforts should be made to stimulate invention and innovation. There is also an urgent need to cut out some of the incredible waste in our system—in both the public and private sectors—engendered by abundant, cheap energy in the past. Rampant consumerism will have to be replaced by serious rather than cosmetic conservation. But the result won't be a return to rapid growth. That phase of the world's history is behind us.

The idea of reindustrialization could be made meaningful by tempering it with a heavy dose of realism. While rejuvenation of America's industrial base might be necessary, it won't produce the rising standard of living which Etzioni and his supporters assume. The emphasis in public policy has to be on equity as well as efficiency. That means, in practical terms, a set of policies which will ensure that no group suffers unduly from the end of economic growth while others continue to add to their wealth in spite of it.

American Attitudes Toward Economic Growth

How do Americans feel about economic growth? A major corporation, Union Carbide, has said they're for it—overwhelmingly!

Their pronouncement was based on a poll conducted for the chemical company. A summary of the survey findings was published in several widely circulated newspapers.

Most respondents—83 percent—said they favored a "fair amount to a great deal" of growth. Another 11 percent favored growth but "not too much." Only 2 percent said they wanted no growth at all. So there you have it. The majority has spoken. If the public wants growth, Union Carbide implies, it should have growth. But how? Americans, they say, see "technology and business as forces for growth."

Mobil Oil carries on a continuous public relations campaign. Its editorial advertisement in the April 20, 1980, *Washington Post* mentioned a National Coalition for Growth. This was described as a "diverse group of educators and foundations united . . . to pause and reflect on the need for growth . . . and the robust business activity needed to make growth possible."

What are these corporations after? The Union Carbide survey gives some clues. Most respondents favor a cut in business taxes. They also would like to see "more accountability for the economic effects of government regulation." Union Carbide officials surely wouldn't be offended if this were interpreted to mean less regulation.

The Carbide survey and Mobil's advertisements are part of a broader anti-regulation campaign. Specific targets are environmental, trucking, and safety regulations. While the campaign is clearly self-serving, corporations have every right to lobby for or against government regulation. Only the utterly naive, however, will believe they're doing it in "the public interest." Carbide suggests that the "growth-no growth" debate has been settled, presumably by its survey. "The issue now is how America's policy-makers can point the nation toward the economic growth its people want."

A major fallacy in big business's pro-growth campaign is the assumption that the sharp decline in economic growth is entirely the result of high business taxes, government regulation, and other "interferences" with free enterprise. Carefully documented studies show that environmental and safety legislation have adversely affected the growth rate. They also show that only a fraction of the decline in economic growth can be attributed to government regulation. As noted throughout this volume, more important causes lie elsewhere.

Another fallacy inherent in the corporations' public relations efforts is that growth can go on forever—that there are no natural barriers to sustained high growth rates. This simply isn't so. As an economy matures, its real costs of production rise. The amounts of time, energy, and other resources needed to produce a given unit of output increase.

Policy makers could stimulate a short burst of accelerated growth by giving businesses all sorts of investment incentives to produce more now. But a faster growth rate couldn't last. We would be borrowing from the future to increase present consumption. Such a policy would be much like an old man having a goat gland operation to stretch his libidinous horizon. The implantation of goat glands might briefly brighten his golden years, but the operation wouldn't start him growing again.

It's not surprising that the public supports economic growth. Americans have been misled for years by conventional economists into believing that the answer to all economic problems is growth and more growth. But an economic system is like an organism—it's not a perpetual motion machine. An economy, like everything else, goes through a life cycle. The American economy reached its growth peak in the 1960s. One consequence was serious environmental damage. Subsequent environmental protection legislation has been only one of many causes of slow growth since the early 1970s, and far from the most important. The most important has been, quite simply, the law of diminishing returns. This is one law that can't be repealed.

Asking the respondents to a public opinion poll if they favor economic growth is an exercise in fatuity. The results are totally predictable. Raising this question is tantamount to asking: "Would you like to live happily ever after?" One can be certain that at least 83 percent of the respondents would reply with a resounding "yes!"

Optimism As a Growth Stimulant

Are businessmen, workers, and consumers cheered by optimistic forecasts? Will such forecasts stimulate investment, encourage people to work harder, buy more—will they, in brief, generate future prosperity? That might be the thinking behind the reports of some perpetually optimistic prognosticators. An example is a forecast of the 1980s published at the start of the decade by the Kiplinger organization. It wasn't just optimistic; it was euphoristic, one of the few medium-term forecasts to suggest that the 1980s will be almost as good a decade as the 1960s.

The conditions that caused robust growth in the 1960s aren't coming back in the 1980s, however. The early 1960s was a period of declining energy prices, full employment, stable consumer prices, and the most rapid economic growth the nation has known. But "stagflation"—the economists' term for high unemployment rates coexisting with inflation—started in the late 1960s, one of the consequences of a declining national growth rate.

Although the U.S. growth rate has dropped sharply since 1969, the decline hasn't been uniform across the country. During the 1970s, for example, per capita income—in constant dollars—went up at annual rates of 1.4 percent in Connecticut, 1.9 percent in New Jersey, and only 0.5 percent in New York. Meanwhile, there were annual increases of 4.5 percent in Kentucky, 4 percent in Louisiana, 3.6 percent in Oklahoma, 3.7 percent in Texas, 3.9 percent in West Virginia, and more than 5 percent in Wyoming.

The Northeastern states were hit hard by rising energy prices. All of the states which experienced large gains in real per capita income produce energy. The Kiplinger staff evidently missed those income shifts. They implied in their forecast that the shift in economic activity from the Snow Belt to the Sun Belt would somehow be reversed during the 1980s, but didn't explain why or how that would happen. There is, of course, no reason why it should. The trend of a half century was simply accelerated by rapidly rising energy prices. There is no reason why that long-term trend should be reversed.

Not many forecasters view the 1980s optimistically. Most anticipate a continuation of the trends of the 1970s, and those were anything but encouraging. Slow national growth will continue to have regional consequences. States producing energy and raw materials have had below-average per capita incomes historically. The industrial states and financial centers of the Northeast have had above-average incomes. Before the end of the century, however, it is likely that their relative positions will be switched. Many states in the South and the West will be above average, while some of the older industrial states will drop below that average.

Can't the trends of the past half century be reversed? Don't they depend, in the final analysis, on government policy? Federal policy might affect the rate of change—it could slow down the decline of the Northeast and the growth of the South and West, but political power shifts with population and income. The Northeast doesn't have the political clout it had fifty years ago. That of the South and West has become stronger. These shifts alone support the view that federal policies are not likely to affect the long-term trends.

The Kiplinger organization doesn't stand alone in its optimism. There must be a market for cheerful prognostication. It might even be good for morale. But do businessmen base their plans on euphoristic forecasts? Apparently not. Although there was a sharp change in the political climate during the early 1980s, which clearly reflected disillusionment with the status quo ante, the economy continued to waffle along as it had been doing for more than a decade.

Resource Scarcity: Truth or Harmless Hyperbole?

Does the world face a problem of resource scarcity? Or do shortages, like beauty, exist only in the eye of the beholder? The latter view was implied by Dr. John Morgan, acting director of the U.S. Bureau of Mines, in an interview with Ben A. Franklin reported in the November 27, 1977, edition of the *New York Times*.

"Shortages are as a culture perceives them," stated Franklin. He went on to quote Dr. Morgan: ". . . as long as we keep up our science and technology, pointing the way to using lower grade ores, the world has more resources now than ever, and there will be even more in the future." Such pronouncements doubtless lift the spirits of optimists who already believe that the only barriers to Utopia are human weakness, political ineptitude, and corporate cupidity. They have one unfortunate defect, however; they simply aren't true.

Perhaps Morgan intended to indulge in harmless hyperbole, but as it stands his statement is misleading. There might be more *known* resources today than in the past; there might even be more recoverable resources. But there are not now, and there will not be in the future, more total non-renewable resources. Indeed, in per capita terms—the only meaningful way to view the world's resource base—supplies of non-renewable resources are constantly dwindling.

In a world characterized by relative peace, "reasonable price incentives and a continuing effort in technological development," Morgan continued, "we're not going to run out of anything." This is a true statement, with or without the conditions imposed. The last barrel of oil, the last ton of coal, or the last unit of any other non-renewable resource will never be produced. Long before any resource is completely used up, the real cost of producing the last unit will become so high, relative to its value, that efforts to extract it would be uneconomical. When it requires more of a given resource—say a ton of coal—to produce another, that resource will not be produced. What matters today is that after decades, or even generations, of stable and declining production costs, there has been a turnaround in the economics of resource exploitation. Virtually all non-renewable natural resources are now produced under rising cost conditions.

Readily available resources are the first to be extracted. In most cases low-cost resources have been depleted. Now we are forced to use more capital and other resources for exploration, to dig and drill deeper, and to develop new techniques for extraction. As a result, costs rise. New methods of mining and drilling also use more energy than those of the past, and the cost of energy is rising faster than other production costs. Technological optimists—who have a penchant for wishful thinking—hope that a breakthrough will ease this situation. There is nothing on the horizon, however, to suggest that relief from further increases in energy prices is likely.

The difficulty with pronouncements such as those quoted by Franklin is that they ignore the economic side of the resource issue. The concepts of scarcity and choice are at the very heart of economics. Yet many economists lost sight of scarcity during the robustly growing 1960s. Events of the 1970s made some of us realize how transitory that period of rapid growth was. In the longer sweep of history, the 1960s will appear as a bright but very brief blip.

Why get excited about all this? Does it matter what our perceptions of scarcity are? Unfortunately, the perceptions of officeholders, and their advisers, determine public policies. And those policies affect all our lives. The dominant view in Washington—under the Reagan administration, as it was during the Carter administration—is that the nation is going through a difficult "period of transition." No one bothers to point out that the nation is always going through a period of transition. Instead, we have had a plethora of proposals to get the economy back on the desired track of full employment without inflation. In the past these involved tinkering with the demand side of the economic equation. Under the Reagan administration the supply-siders took over. Their prescription was to increase production in the private sector so that prices would fall and employment would rise. But the supply-siders paid no more attention to resource constraints than their demand-side brethren. Both propose to deal with symptoms rather than acknowledging the basic cause of the nation's economic *malaise*.

Few officeholders are willing to risk public displeasure by acknowledging that supply constraints contribute in an important way to economic problems. The reason? There's not much that can be done about supply constraints, except to adjust aspirations downward. One can understand why politicians ignore this dismal conclusion, but that doesn't mean it will go away.

None of this means the American economy is on the brink of disaster. But the nation will have to adjust to a new set of circumstances. Politicians will have to abandon old habits of thought, and view the world as it is, not as they wish it might be, if unemployment and inflation are to be dealt with realistically.

Keynesian policies adopted after World War II showed that the nation could cope with the demand deficiencies that had caused the depression of the 1930s. If resources and energy were available in unlimited quantities, it would be easy to handle any remaining demand problems. But they aren't. Assurances that science and technology will somehow make resources more abundant make cheerful reading. But they only delay the day when officeholders will have to face the problems of resource scarcity as squarely as they faced the problem of inadequate demand in the past.

The Effects of an Aging Population

In *The Wealth of Nations* Adam Smith described the advantages of the division of labor. Specialization and exchange, he wrote, increase production and output per person. Smith's observations are as valid today as they were when he wrote them. But economists have carried specialization too far and haven't been interested enough in exchange—especially in the realm of ideas.

Many economists pay no attention to what's happening to population. The study of population, they believe, is the province of demographers. Technical studies should, of course, be left to properly trained specialists. But the results of demographic studies—and readily available population data—should be used by economists because population changes have definite impacts on the economy.

One of the more significant population changes is in its age distribution. Table 3 summarizes recent changes.

The first two age groups are declining. This has reduced the demand for children's shoes, clothing, baby food, and toys. The next two age groups—15 to 24—which include students and new labor force entrants, bulged by more than 11 million during the period shown. But the growth of the 15 to 19 group is tapering off. It will drop quite rapidly during the 1980s. The 20 to 24 group is still growing; but as the "cohort" behind moves into it, the number in this age bracket also will decline.

The youth market—broadly defined to include everyone from 15 to 24—has been expanding. Purveyors of fast foods, rock-music albums, blue-jeans, and other youth items, have prospered. Entrepreneurs who "create" demand have to keep up with the changing age distributions. But the youth era is slipping by. The number of 15- to 24-year-olds in the labor force peaked in 1980 at about 25 million. By 1990, however, this age group will be down to 22 million and declining. Meanwhile, the 25 to 44 group will increase from 47 million in 1980 to 61 million in 1990.

Table 3

**Age Distribution in the U.S.
1964-1980**

Age Group	Percent of Total Population	
	1964	*1980*
Under 5	11	7
5 to 14	22	15
15 to 19	7	9
20 to 24	7	9
25 to 44	24	28
45 to 64	20	20
65 and over	9	11
Total	100	100

Source: U.S. Bureau of the Census.

The changing age distribution will have some predictable effects, but we can only speculate about others. One conclusion seems inescapable: There will be a pronounced drop in college and university enrollments. This will be caused partly by a decline in student-age population. But the escalating cost of higher education, and diminishing job opportunities in education and other fields with a surplus of college graduates, will contribute to the trend.

There should be good news as well. Many of the nation's unemployed have been concentrated in the under-24 group. Numerous "entry jobs" of the past have been eliminated by technological change. The labor force will grow—from 105 million at the end of 1980 to 116 million in 1990—but there will be a smaller number of youngsters competing for available entry jobs.

The smallest changes will be in the 45 to 65 group, which has been a constant share of the population since the mid-sixties. About 33 million persons in this age group were in the work force in 1980. By 1990 that number will have increased by at least 2 million.

The big bulge will be in the "prime" working ages of 25 to 44. This group will grow from about 47 million in 1980 to 61 million in 1990. Here is where the competition for jobs and promotions will be most intense. This age bracket will include a large proportion of persons with post-high-school education. Unless the economic growth rate picks up smartly—which is not likely—or there is a pronounced shift toward more labor-intensive activities, the chances that this age group will maintain its favorable employment and unemployment records aren't good. The number and proportion of persons past 65 will continue to rise steadily. Now that mandatory retirement at 65 has been outlawed, many workers will remain—or try to remain—in the active labor force. That will, of course, exacerbate the problems of those in the "prime" age group.

As noted above, not all of the effects of the changing age distribution can be anticipated. A few things, however, seem certain: In one way or another, the changing age distribution will profoundly affect higher education, patterns of employment, and what we now call "life styles." If the changes are profound enough, they might even affect the way we are governed.

Are There Limits to Growth?

The prescription of faster growth as a cure-all for the nation's economic problems calls to mind a demented parent berating his twenty-five-year old son for not growing. The only way a mature person can grow is to grow fat. That's a lot like inflation. Such growth can be deleterious to health.

A lucid and sensible discussion of growth appeared in the September 1978 issue of the *American Journal of Physics*. In an article entitled "Forgotten Fundamentals of the Energy Crisis," Albert A. Bartlett, of the Department of Physics and Astrophysics at the University of Colorado, demonstrates convincingly that growth can't solve our problems since we live in a finite environment.

Bartlett dramatizes his point by discussing the growth of bacteria in a bottle. Bacteria grow by division, and they grow fast. If a single bacterium with a "dividing time" of one minute is placed in a bottle, the bacteria will grow exponentially—that is, they'll follow the "compound interest" law of growth. Assume that the first bacterium is deposited at 11 a.m., and that the bottle is full at noon. The principle illustrated by this example is the acceleration of growth.

At 11:54 a.m.—90 percent of the elapsed time—the bottle would be only 1/64th (or 1.5 percent) full. Two minutes later it would be 1/16th (6 percent) full. At 11:58 a.m. it would be one-fourth full—at 11:59 a.m., half full. At noon it would be completely full!

If the point of this example seems ambiguous, look at a chart of energy consumption in the United States since 1850. It's an exponential growth curve. Or look at a chart of U.S. Gross National Product in current dollars since, say, 1940. It's another exponential growth curve. World population is also growing exponentially, and it would be easy to give numerous other examples. Exponential growth means that whatever is growing doubles in a given time period.

If one knows the growth rate of anything, "doubling time" can be calculated by a simple formula: $D = 70/r$, where r is the rate of growth. For example, if you deposit $100 at 10 percent, compounded continuously, it will double in seven years. At 7 percent it will double in ten years, and so on. This formula can be applied to anything that grows at a constant rate.

This formula can also be used to determine whether a growth rate is increasing or decreasing. If the consumer price index doubled over one ten-year period, then doubled again in five years, the rate of inflation is increasing. But if output per worker doubled over a twenty-year period, for example, then doubled again over a forty-year period, productivity would be declining.

Bartlett shows that when we increase our consumption of anything at 7 percent per year, the amount consumed in one decade is approximately equal to all previous consumption. During the 1960s, for example, the consumption of electricity in the United States increased 7 percent annually. The nation consumed as much electricity in that one decade as it had consumed since the first spark of electrical energy was put on the market.

Petroleum was first used as a fuel in this country around 1880. The consumption of oil then grew exponentially until the 1920s. It leveled off for a decade or so as natural gas took over part of the market. Between 1940 and 1974, however, the consumption of oil in the United States followed the compound-interest growth law again.

Geologists tell us that we have used about half of the known domestic oil reserve. At first blush this sounds encouraging. We still have half of our oil left, and it took ninety-eight years to use the other half. But if we deplete those reserves at 7 percent a year, they'll be gone in a decade. If the rate of consumption drops to 4 percent, the oil reserve would last a bit less than eighteen years. In terms of Bartlett's bacteria example, we're at 11:59 a.m. on the "growth clock," even at the lower consumption rate. It's not all that long until noon.

There's a great deal of public impatience with such gloomy prognoses. In spite of nearly a decade of economic stagnation and growing inflation, most economists remain optimistic about the long-term future. Politicians seem to believe they have to promise better days ahead, but they don't tell us what they base those promises on. We really can't continue to ignore the laws of arithmetic, however, as do those afflicted by growthmania.

What's to be gained by such gloomy talk? We're not bacteria living in a bottle. True, but we live in a finite environment. The purpose of Bartlett's clever illustration is to stress the need for conservation of energy and resources. That, in turn, means giving up the habits that have made America the most profligate wastrel of energy and resources in the world.

It doesn't mean going back to the life style of the 1870s, but it does mean giving up the unrealistic vision of a life of ease and plenty for everyone. The truth is, the century ahead will be a difficult time, with world population growing, energy supplies diminishing, food becoming more expensive, and resources becoming increasingly difficult and costly to exploit.

Bartlett's article should be made required reading in high schools and colleges. It's not a scare story. It simply points out the facts. One of these is that it's impossible to violate the most elementary—but incontrovertible—of all scientific principles, the laws of arithmetic.

Economics: Inside Looking Out—Outside Looking In

Two themes have been woven into the discussion of this volume. One is that the industrial nations of the world entered an era of slow growth at the end of the 1960s, and that this is not a transitory change. The second is that conventional economics hasn't recognized this fundamental change. The standard fare fed to unsuspecting students in economics courses is that growth is not only desirable, it is the "normal" economic condition. Any time an economy slips backward, therefore, it's because the system isn't being properly managed or is the victim of some malevolent "external" force.

The statement about "management" requires clarification. It's easy to see how totalitarian economies are managed. But who "manages" a private enterprise economy like ours? The federal government tries, to some extent, through monetary and fiscal policies. But it's clear that those policies haven't worked for at least ten years. Traditional economists, whether they focus on demand or production stimuli, still believe that federal authorities simply haven't found the right combination of monetary and fiscal levers to pull. They can't accept the views of a few mavericks who say it doesn't matter because those levers aren't hooked to the basic causes of contemporary economic problems.

Professional economics journals are filled with articles about growth. But sooner or later one of the more alert business publications had to recognize the true state of affairs. If there were an award for perceptivity in business journalism, it should have gone to *Business Week*. The feature article in the January 28, 1980, issue was entitled "The Shrinking Standard of Living." The authors failed to get at the fundamental causes of this phenomenon, but they deserve praise for recognizing a problem which most economists refuse to acknowledge.

For three decades, the authors pointed out, Americans enjoyed a steadily rising standard of living. A generation of Americans has known no other economic condition. "But," they said, "the golden age of the consumer is over. The U.S. standard of living is shrinking." And while the optimism of most economists remains intact, that of the public—the writers asserted—is "shattered." One consequence, they believe, is that "the battle over income shares will intensify."

A short article concerned with the living standards of other democratic, industrialized nations accompanied the feature story. There also the outlook is bleak. So the problem of slow or no growth isn't uniquely American. Other countries are facing the same difficulties. On the editorial page the *Business Week* editors explained why they believe the industrial nations of the Western world have reached their present sorry state. Though three distinct reasons were given, all are in fact interrelated.

The major cause of the problem, as the editors see it, is the "predatory" pricing policy of the international oil cartel. This has had a depressing effect on capital spending, because higher energy costs have "upset the traditional returns on investments." Finally, productivity has increased only slowly, and this is partly a result of inadequate investment.

The diagnosis of the *Business Week* analysts is excellent. It takes a certain amount of nerve for a business publication to state hard, cold, and unpleasant facts bluntly. Some high-priced business advisory letters have denied that anything is basically wrong with the American economy. They have projected instead a great boom in investment and consumer spending in the 1980s. Such forecasts are wishful thinking.

Did the *Business Week* editors have a prescription for dealing with the problem? In fact, they did. First, they advised us, the U.S. must reduce its dependency on foreign oil. Most economic analysts would accept this proposal, although for a wide variety of reasons. But the rest of their prescription is disappointing. It's based entirely on traditional economics—the brand that has been unable to give any useful policy advice for more than a decade.

Specifically, the editors said the government must "maintain strict monetary and fiscal policies to slow the pace of inflation." Tax laws, they continued, must be revised "to encourage investment and promote productivity." They conclude that there is "no other way to raise real income and start the standard of living climbing again." So, in the final analysis, the editors haven't made a break with the past. They, too, accept Disney's First Law that "Wishing Will Make It So!"

It's a pity that an excellent diagnosis failed to produce a realistic and innovative prescription. The beginning of this section suggested that one of the nation's more influential business publications had finally come to terms with reality. Perhaps it's even more unrealistic, however, to expect a business-oriented publication to abandon the dogma that faster economic growth is the answer to the nation's problems. The changes that have been going on for more than a decade aren't transitory, however, and no combination of monetary and fiscal policies, which were designed to keep short-term fluctuations within narrow bounds in a robustly growing economy, will curb inflation in a no-growth economy. And a tax reduction, such as that initiated by the Reagan administration, will not get at the basic problem. All it will do eventually is add to the well-being of those who remain prosperous even in a stagnant economy.

Reducing dependence on imported oil won't reduce energy costs, but it should be done for political and military reasons. Energy costs will continue to rise, no matter what alternative sources are developed to replace imports. So the living standards of a "cheap energy" era are gone, and they're gone for good. There's no point in dragging out old bromides to stimulate growth. What the nation needs is a new set of policies to "manage" the no–growth economy which is either upon us or a short distance down the road.

Americans have much to be concerned about, as do the citizens of other mature industrialized societies. There has even been a change in the attitudes of some of the more serious professional "futurists." They appear to be less ebullient, more restrained in their optimism, than they or their predecessors were ten years ago. They are more willing to talk about pollution, overcrowding, and resource scarcities than one used to hear from modern-day counterparts of the augurs of Rome. They remain firm in their faith that science and technology will rescue us from the contemporary doldrums. But that faith might not be quite as strong as it was at the beginning of the "stagnant seventies."

Old-style space age forecasts are becoming somewhat rare. Even the more optimistic futurists say less about rocket travel among automated cities covered by geodesic domes. The idea of progress remains so firmly ingrained in their thinking, however, that they continue to project rising standards of living—however small the increases might be.

Other commentators—definitely not members of the futurist fraternity—are taking a more realistic view. In the November 1979 issue of *Smithsonian*, Sam Love asked: "Whatever became of the predicted effortless world?" He recalled projections made a half-century ago by Norman Bel Geddes, Charles Steinmetz, R. M. Langer, and others who thought energy would become so abundant it would be sold at low flat rates (as water was then) because it wouldn't pay to install meters. With cheap energy, mankind would have at its disposal a limitless array of mechanical servants. Who echoes that view today?

Even more impressive, in the same issue of *Smithsonian*, are several evocative cartoons by Robert Osborn. His clever caricatures lampoon our self-indulgence, our prodigal waste of electricity, "the internal combustion engine [as] an all-day sucker we crave," and so on. One cartoon depicts mankind's disbelief "at the emptying cornucopia." In the last one "the material objects of our too-easy life flow in a torrent . . . down the drain."

The insights of cartoonists (like Osborn) and satirists (like Art Buchwald) are in closer touch with reality than those of many eminent scholars. One won't learn much about the changing world by reading today's scholarly journals. Most economists have abandoned the real world for the safer terrain of abstract mathematical models. Some sociologists are no better off; they're worrying about the "*anomie*" (their term for *malaise*) engendered by material progress at a time when such progress is on the wane. Only bioeconomists—a small dissident sect whose views are ignored by traditionalists—will be in sympathy with Osborn's powerful cartoons.

The next few decades will be an extension of the recent past. By the turn of the century there will be fewer private cars in use. We should, by then, have made some progress on a public transportation system. As energy costs spiral upward we'll substitute labor for mechanical processes where it's technically and economically feasible. Some operations—steel mills and coal conversion plants, for example—have to be large to be efficient. But many manufacturing processes can function well on a small scale. So we're likely to see a mix of more small and fewer large enterprises.

Instead of the "effortless world" projected in the 1930s, there will be more household self-sufficiency. The neglected arts of home-cooking, canning, sewing, and baking will be revived. Many purely cosmetic services will be priced out of existence. Needless packaging and useless style changes will be eliminated without any loss in the real standard of living.

The near-term future as seen by bioeconomists isn't one of economic disaster; it will be one of adaptation as a larger population presses ever harder on declining energy and resource bases. With foresight, and democratic planning, we can adjust to slowly declining living standards as easily as we did to the explosive growth in real income that followed World War II.

The real uncertainties of the rest of this century won't be economic—they'll be political. In a world where regressive rulers can inflame the minds of impressionable subjects—even in a few small, poor, and militarily weak countries—anything can happen, and probably will. A reasonable answer to terrorist tactics and flagrant violations of international law is world government powerful enough to enforce that law. But more powerful world government would mean diminution of national power. However urgent the need for such power shifts, only a mindless optimist would expect them to occur soon.

If the democratic societies of the world survive global political debacles in reasonably good shape, there will still be plenty of economic worries. The probability of political disaster is greater than that of economic collapse. But the likelihood of little or no economic growth—with some redistribution of income and wealth from rich to poor regions, and rich to poor nations—is greater than the likelihood that some technological miracle will bring back the rapid growth of the past.

Economic Growth—The Global View

Scientists and mathematicians often approach an unsolved problem by relating it to an analogous problem that has been solved. They apply a method that has proved itself in the past to the new problem. Reasoning by analogy is valid, provided there is similarity between two problems. If not, some other approach or some other analogy has to be sought.

Economists approach problems in the same way, but it's easier to be led astray by false analogies in economics than in the more rigorous disciplines. Some economic policies have worked in the past, but they won't work today because conditions have changed. Nowhere is this more evident than in the field of development economics. The objective of this branch of economics is to find ways to transform underdeveloped countries so that they will resemble developed countries. The goal is to stimulate rapid economic growth and "structural change." The means of reaching this goal is to lessen dependence on agriculture while stimulating the growth of indigenous industry. Achieving that objective, however, is something else.

Since 1944 the International Monetary Fund and World Bank have attempted to raise living standards in the underdeveloped countries. With a few notable exceptions, such as Taiwan, progress has been slow. In fact, progress has been stopped in many places by rapidly rising energy prices.

The United Nations has held numerous conferences on economic development. One was held in New Delhi in February 1980. Its main outcome was to demonstrate that the developed and underdeveloped countries of the world have reached an impasse. Spokesmen for developed countries said the introduction of political issues prevented a consensus. The "Group of 77," as the underdeveloped countries are sometimes called (although their number has grown to 119), maintain that the developed countries have grown rich by exploiting the world's poor nations. Now, they say, the developed nations are unwilling to share.

What do the less developed countries (LDCs), as they are now euphemistically called, want? First, a global fund of $300 billion to help them industrialize. Their goal, announced at the Lima conference of 1975, is to increase their share of the world's industrial output from 7 percent to 25 percent by the end of the century. Representatives of the developed nations contend that the new fund would duplicate efforts of the International Monetary Fund and World Bank.

The World Bank's reports are fascinating documents. They contain enormous amounts of global data. But the most interesting sections deal with development strategy. One wouldn't guess from the 1979 report, for example, that there are energy and materials shortages which might limit growth and development.

The theory behind the World Bank's strategy, as enunciated in the 1979 report, provides a straightforward development formula. First, invest in agricultural machinery to "release" labor for a growing manufacturing sector. Later, as personal incomes rise, a growing share of the work force will provide professional and personal services. The key to this process is increasing productivity. A critical element is sound management.

What's wrong with this formula? It worked in the past. This strategy would replicate the way the United States and other developed nations reached their present status. The same process occurred in centrally-controlled as well as in capitalist societies. So, if the process isn't affected by political systems, what's to keep it from working in today's weaker countries?

There are two obstacles which didn't exist when today's developed countries were themselves underdeveloped. First, until a decade ago, developing countries had access to abundant, low-cost energy. Also, relatively few countries had become industrialized by the middle of the present century. Between countries producing raw materials and those producing fabricated products there was a balance which permitted steadily expanding international trade. Unfortunately, the balance wasn't stable because the industrialized countries grew wealthy while the producers of raw materials remained poor.

Before World War II many underdeveloped countries were colonies of one of the industrialized nations. In other cases, industrialists owned raw materials in nominally free countries. But one of the provisions of the United Nations charter was the abolition of colonialism. Dozens of new independent countries replaced the former colonies. Most were included in the original Group of 77. As other countries gained their independence, the ranks of the underdeveloped lands grew. They've gained political clout, but they're not making it on the economic front.

One group of formerly poor nations has been shifted to a new category, "capital surplus oil exporters," which includes Saudi Arabia, Libya, and Kuwait. The other members of OPEC are still regarded as underdeveloped, although they are part of another new category—the middle-income countries—to distinguish them from the thirty-seven hard-core, low-income countries.

Much of the organization for international development took place during the buoyant 1960s when the industrialized countries— whether free-market or planned—were growing robustly. But growth rates have dropped sharply in the largest industrial nations, especially the United States and Russia. It's easy to be generous to the have-nots when your own real income is climbing. It gets progressively harder as your real income levels off—or possibly begins to decline.

Does this mean that the present pattern of world economic development will remain more or less frozen? Or will the rich get richer and the poor get poorer? Neither conclusion necessarily follows. It is becoming increasingly clear, however, that the standard model of economic development, based on the history of today's industrialized countries, might not be working anymore. Future economic developments might be quite unlike those of the past.

The World Bank expects population to increase by 1.1 billion persons, or 27 percent, between 1976 and 1990. But exports of fuels and energy are projected to rise 52 percent, with no change in the relative shares between industrialized and developing countries. Raw material exports are expected to go up 58 percent—again with no change in relative shares. But the Bank's staff looks for a major increase of 159 percent in manufacturing exports. They project the LDC's share to grow from 9.5 percent to 16 percent of the world total, and the industrialized countries' share to decline from 81 percent to 76 percent.

To summarize, the World Bank expects the energy and raw materials "pies" to be half again as big in 1990 as they were in 1976. The manufactured goods pie is expected to be one and one-half times larger. Since the world's population will increase by a bit more than one-fourth, the Bank's staff projects healthy increases in per capita income. The largest increases, they believe, will come in the LDCs.

Like other optimists, the authors of the Bank's report see the energy problem as a "transitional" one. By the end of the century, they realize, there will be more reliance on sources other than petroleum. Without describing how alternative sources will be developed—or how future energy costs will compare with those which stimulated economic development in the pre-OPEC era—they don't see energy supply constraints holding back further industrialization.

A concern expressed in the Bank's 1979 report is that individual countries will pull back from an expansive trade policy. It warns against import substitution under which countries try to meet their own needs. If individual countries reduce imports, they also must reduce growth. This, of course, would slow the growth of the world economy. What the world needs, the report's authors say, is more, not less, international trade.

It's easy to design a model of expanding world trade. The LDCs will industrialize by producing low-technology goods, such as clothing and footwear. With earnings from export sales to high-technology nations, such as the United States, they will buy computers, helicopters, and so forth. It's hard to argue against this model in principle. After all, it's based on Adam Smith's first economic dictum—the surest way to achieve prosperity is to specialize and exchange.

But Adam Smith was a rationalist. His economic system assumes that everyone will behave rationally. If we did, there would be no trade barriers. There would also be no wars, or even the threat of wars with the excessive military spending which this entails. But as long as the threat of war persists, individual nations will protect the industries they would need in case of actual hostilities.

It's unlikely that industrial exports will more than double from 1976 to 1990. The World Bank's development strategy doesn't pay enough attention to the most important changes that occurred during the 1970s; namely, growing shortages of materials and energy. The Bank sees the necessity of increased production of fuels, energy, and raw materials. But the reason for this—apart from the need to feed and

clothe a growing world population—is to permit rapid industrialization of the LDCs while allowing slower growth in developed
countries.

Economists use the term "shortage" in a relative sense. So a
shortage of anything means the price of that thing will rise faster than
other prices. The greater the shortage, the faster the rise in price.

People can live without a lot of manufactured products. But they
can't live without food, fuel, clothing, and housing. The most
important developments during the remainder of this century will be
increased efficiency in the production of food, fibers, and fuels. Rising
prices will force conservation of the earth's steadily dwindling energy
dowry. That will require a reversal of past trends.

The conventional model of economic development, which the
World Bank accepts without reservation, is one in which an increasing
share of the world's labor force is devoted to providing services. To
suggest that this model of the past will apply to the future is to ignore
the scarcity signals which are already loud and clear. The projected
growth of world output beggars belief.

Nations which can produce a surplus of food, fuels, and fiber
during the years ahead will prosper. Those which have to import some
or all of these items will experience relative declines in per capita
income. The old terms of trade which favored manufacturing will shift
in favor of fuels and raw materials. This process has been going on
within the United States for at least a decade. It will be slower at the
international level, but such shifts are inevitable because they will
reflect changing economic reality. It might take economists a long
time, however, to adjust their models to fit the new reality.

The differences in outlook between the 1979 World Bank report
and the document called *Global 2000*, discussed in Chapter 1, are
startling. The World Bank envisions continued economic growth and
progress. *Global 2000* contains a grim warning of a world that will be
increasingly crowded, hungry, polluted, and unstable by the year
2000—unless international action heads off the problems. One of the
conclusions in *Global 2000* is incontrovertible. The problems of an
already crowded planet, with a dwindling energy and resource base,
can only be approached on an international basis. So the agency that

should be involved is the United Nations. In a rational and compassionate world the U.N. would be given authority to do what is needed to cope with the deteriorating global economic situation—at the expense of national sovereignty if necessary. Unfortunately, even moderately optimistic projections of growth and development in the LDCs, such as those made by the World Bank, are likely to retard rather than accelerate a rational and unified approach for coping with the problems of global poverty.

Science and Pseudo-Science

Politicians, consumer advocates, futurists, and spokesmen for other constituencies use the word "solve" with reckless abandon. The truth is, we don't solve social or economic problems; we accommodate or adapt to them. But many writers continue to imply that a future generation will solve the problems that plague us today.

In mathematics and the physical sciences, problems are solved by logical proofs or by demonstration. Dr. Jonas Salk, for example, solved the problem of polio by developing a vaccine that created an immunity to the disease. That is problem-solving at its best.

Until a half-century ago, mathematicians believed all mathematical problems—including some that had remained unsolved for generations—would eventually be solved. In 1931, however, a twenty-five-year old Austrian mathematician, Kurt Gödel, published a complex paper on "undecidable theory" which proved conclusively that entire classes of mathematical problems can't be "solved," in the traditional meaning of that word. While Gödel achieved undying fame among mathematicians, his name isn't a household word. His death, in January 1978, didn't receive the prominent notice given to that of other eminent scientists. But Gödel's contribution was as important to mathematics, many believe, as Einstein's was to physics.

Even some mathematicians had difficulty understanding Gödel's original work. But a short book, *Gödel's Proof* by Ernest Nagel and James R. Newman (New York University Press, 1958), translates his complex ideas into language a mathematical neophyte can understand. Although this book is far from easy, the reward of reading it is worth the effort.

Why should an economist be interested in the complexities of mathematics? Because economists could learn a lot from undecidable theory. If there are classes of abstract problems that can't be solved in the conventional sense, aren't we presumptuous to think that the far more complex problems of the real would can be solved? Asking this question is not raising a straw man. As long as the public is misled into thinking that economic problems can be "solved," in the sense of getting back to "the good old days"—itself an illusory notion—society will not make the changes needed to adapt to new conditions. And it is far more realistic to think in terms of adaptation or adjustment to new conditions than it is to believe in mankind's infinite capacity to "solve" complex problems.

Among the most egregious of the "problem-solvers" are the pop-futurists. One of the best known of these is Alvin Toffler, whose lucubrations about a new age of abundance were described in *The Third Wave* (William Morrow & Co., 1980), a widely touted futuristic book. For the busy reader Toffler squeezed out the essence of *The Third Wave* in a short article, "A New Kind of Man in the Making," in the March 9, 1980, *New York Times Magazine*.

Jerry Pournelle's review in the *Washington Post Book World* (May 4, 1980) was laudatory. But Pournell candidly admitted that Toffler's views correspond closely to his own. He said that "much of Toffler's overview of technology will be familiar to seasoned readers of science fiction." This is superb. Many of us enjoy good science fiction, but most of us try to distinguish between fantasy and reality. As Pournelle correctly indicated, the line between the two in Toffler's book is thin. A second review, in the March 30, 1980, *New York Times Book Review*, by Langdon Winner, an MIT political scientist, is more objective. *The Third Wave*, Winner says, "contains the same kind of titillating but slipshod analysis" as Toffler's earlier *Future Shock*. Toffler tries to describe the history of the world in terms of two great waves. The first was the agricultural revolution which provided the basis for modern civilization. The second was the industrial revolution. What will the third wave be? It's nothing more than the future. But what a future.

Quoting from Winner's review: "Diverse new technical systems, especially those in electronics, genetics, and biology, will replace the banging, clanking, polluting machinery of yesterday. Energy will be derived from a variety of renewable resources. . . . Decision-making will be decentralized, social hierarchies leveled." The evidence for these "brash claims," Winner says, "is less than systematic or convincing." Toffler's "method," if it can be dignified with that scholarly term, is to gather bits and scraps of information, to interview corporate officials, and high-ranking military officers (and to take what they tell him at face value), then assemble this anecdotal material in a "colorful, fast-moving pastiche."

He is also accomplished at cooking up neologisms such as "prosumer" (a consumer of his or her own product), "demassification" (of the media, that is), or the "configuration me" who won't accept the mass-produced "imagery" of today's media but will figure out his or her own images from "broken chips and blips of imagery." There's more of this gibberish, even in the abbreviated article in the *Times Magazine*, and Winner mentions other linguistic abominations such as "techno-rebel," "econ-consciousness," "infosphere," and so on. These terms "are announced with such frequency that the reader soon learns to distrust them."

How is the Third Wave to come about? Nobody knows. Seriously, that's Toffler's answer. He points out that the biosphere can't withstand industrial civilization's unlimited assault, and the age of nonrenewable energy will end. "Beyond this," Winner says, "he has little to say. Those who worry about cause and effect and explanations are, in Mr. Toffler's eyes, hopelessly mired in a Second Wave linear mentality." Anyone who can follow this argument should have no difficulty agreeing with Toffler's conclusions.

Toffler surely doesn't care what a few academics think about his book. He must be secure in the knowledge that his imaginative, if meaningless, prose will augment the wealth he earned from *Future Shock*. One can share Winner's hope, however, that there will indeed be a new future; one in which "sociological popularizers stop counting history in threes and our visions of the future contain more than cheap thrills."

Space Colonization: The Ultimate Answer?

In *The Third Wave* Toffler walks a thin line between reasonable speculation and fantasy, with a heavy list toward the latter. Despite the far-out nature of his prognostications, however, Toffler remains earthbound. Another proposed solution to mankind's future problems, with a distinct science-fiction air, is space colonization. It would require a volume much larger than the present one to do justice to this topic, but it has to be mentioned—however briefly—as part of the futuristic agenda.

The leading exponent of space colonization is Gerard K. O'Neill, whose scientific accomplishments and credentials are beyond question. O'Neill is a high-energy physicist at Princeton University, and his scientific reputation is based on the work he has done in this field. His recognized scientific accomplishments are not related to the ideas he has developed about human colonies in space. The latter grew out of exercises he assigned to undergraduate students at Princeton.

O'Neill's views about space colonization were spelled out in a book called *The High Frontier* (William Morrow and Company, 1977), which is an unusual combination of fiction and biography, coupled with a description of his proposal to colonize space.

Two chapters are devoted to terrestrial problems. O'Neill's discussion of the "human prospect on planet earth" is an excellent, succinct description of mankind's Malthusian dilemma. He is familiar with the limits-to-growth literature, and appears to accept the notion that mankind is at present on a collision course with disaster. But O'Neill is convinced there is an escape valve. Some time before the year 2005, he believes, the first space colony will have been established.

O'Neill's space colonies would be self-contained, and basically self-sufficient, spaceships of varying sizes and configurations. The space habitat he has designated "Island Three" would be one he considers to be of "moderate size." It would have a diameter of four miles, a length of twenty miles, and a total "land" area of 500 square miles. It would, he feels, support a population of several million people. The largest that could be built "within the limits of ordinary, present-day structural materials like iron and aluminum, and with oxygen pressures equal to 5,000 feet above sea level on Earth . . . could have a total land area of as much as seven thousand square miles: about half that of Switzerland."

O'Neill's second fantasy, *2081* (Simon & Shuster), was published in 1981. Like *The High Frontier* it is a peculiar combination of science fiction and what O'Neill refers to as "factual commentary of my own."

O'Neill has a fictional alter ego called Eric C. Rawson. The first part of about two-thirds of the chapters are "written by" E.C.R. in the past tense. Then O'Neill picks up the second part writing in the first person singular. It's a clever technique. Fantasy is smoothly blended with "factual commentary." An unwary reader who knows nothing about economics or physics might believe that O'Neill's fantasized space colonies actually will be spinning around in 2081.

O'Neill's work reminds one a little of the stories by Stanislaw Lem which appear in the *New Yorker*. O'Neill doesn't come close to Lem as a writer, but Lem's stories are full of scientific terminology and some refer to well-known scientists. This creates the illusion that Lem is writing about reality when he is, in fact, writing superb science fiction. Most of Lem's stories are sufficiently bizzare to preclude any confusion with reality. But then he isn't trying to confuse, and his stories don't always have cheerful endings.

There was little initial interest among scientists in O'Neill's proposals. But an article of his dealing with space colonization appeared in the magazine *Physics Today* in 1974. It aroused the interest and support of such luminaries as Carl Sagan and Freeman Dyson. Somehow, however, others have failed to capture the enthusiasm which has sustained O'Neill's dream.

One might have expected a revival of interest in space colonization after the first successful voyages of *Columbia* in 1981. But it didn't materialize. After a few days of national euphoria, following the initial flight, that remarkable accomplishment was displaced in the media by news dealing with more mundane matters. Perhaps the fact that it had cost more than $6 billion to build this spaceship and send it on its first mission had cooled the ardor of some who might have been impressed at one time with the feasibility of constructing habitable space colonies. A reasonable estimate of what it might cost to build

O'Neill's "Island Three"—much less a colony half the size of Switzerland—would surely stagger even the wildest imagination.

Must There Be a Solution?

Nothing is more tenacious than a firmly held belief. One of these is the belief that there *has* to be a way out of the Malthusian dilemma, other than inevitable catastrophe engendered by unrestrained population growth impinging on steadily diminishing stocks of energy and raw materials. That idea, expressed in one form or another, probably comes as close as any other to a near-universal dogma subscribed to by most of the educated inhabitants of the earth. Few would refer to this idea as a dogma, however, since that word is generally associated with religious belief. One who has is David Ehrenfeld in *The Arrogance of Humanism* (Oxford University Press, 1978).

The Arrogance of Humanism is a courageous book which could have been written only by a scientist with impeccable credentials. Its author holds an M.D. from Harvard Medical School and a Ph.D. in zoology from the University of Florida. He describes, then proceeds to demolish with the tools of logic, what the dust jacket calls "a religion gone mad." That "religion" is better known as "humanism." Its tenets are subscribed to consciously or unconsciously by many if not most scientists.

Not all humanists belong to the subgroup known as "secular humanists." But those who do scorn religious beliefs because they are based on "untested assumptions." That, says Ehrenfeld, is precisely what's wrong with humanism. It, too, is based entirely on untested—and untestable—assumptions.

What are these assumptions? Ehrenfeld divides them into two groups. The *primary* assumptions are: (a) all problems can be solved, and (b) all problems can be solved by people. The *secondary* assumptions are: (a) many problems can be solved by technology; (b) those that can't have solutions in the social world (of politics, economics, etc.); (c) the supplies of some resources are infinite; (d) those that aren't have substitutes; (e) when the chips are down we'll work together for a solution; and (f) human civilization will survive.

Taken together, these assumptions imply that man has complete mastery over nature. There's nothing that can't be accomplished by reason, science and money. The ancient Greeks had a word for this attitude—they called it "hubris." Its English counterpart is "insolence" or "arrogance." Hence the title of Ehrenfeld's book.

Ehrenfeld questions the prevailing belief that human intelligence and technology can solve all the world's problems. Nor is this belief benign. Economics is one of the fields infected by humanist beliefs. This might be amusing if the consequences weren't potentially serious. Economics is—by definition—the science of scarcity. The process of economizing is one of choosing among alternatives. The only reason we have to choose is because resources are scarce. In Utopia—if this earthly paradise could ever be achieved—there would be no need for economists.

Something has happened to the majority of economists, however. They are among the most vocal "technological optimists" who promise us that solutions to today's problems are on the way. They believe that scarcity is no longer a key issue. As Ehrenfeld points out, they subscribe to the myth that there will always be a substitute for anything that becomes "really" scarce.

Ellen Goodman, the Boston columnist, has written a delightful parody showing how specious the belief in infinite substitutability can be. She talks about conditions in 1995, when gasohol has given way to 100 percent alcohol to propel the automobiles which Americans seem to be unable to do without. There's no grain left over for food (or drink), but "in November every year, people gave thanks because their tank runneth over."

It's impossible in a short space to do justice to Ehrenfeld's book. Anyone with a serious interest in the future of mankind should read it. It's not a perfect book, but perfection is rare. What matters is its central message. It is one every serious person should carefully ponder. It urges us to preserve "those human strengths that even humanism cannot eliminate."

Ehrenfeld's dispassionate analysis of humanism should not be confused in any way with the attack on modern science by the Moral

Majority and other fundamentalists. Ehrenfeld *is* a scientist, and it would be calumny of the worst kind to even imply that his views lend support to anti-evolutionists or others of that ilk. What his book makes clear, however, is that the humanists are as dogmatic in their belief that science will ultimately "solve" mankind's problems as the fundamentalists are in their belief that science will lead man astray.

Ehrenfeld's message is not one of despair. He has warned us against the false prophets who promise an unattainable Utopia. The alternative isn't a bleak or drab future or—far worse—imminent catastrophe. It is one, however, in which realistic expectations of what science and technology can do for mankind are tempered by an awareness of the problems engendered by scarcity—problems that cannot be made to disappear by wishful thinking, or pseudo-scientific prognosticating.

Society doesn't need more scientists, economists, or others who promise Utopia. What it could use is more Ellen Goodmans, Art Buchwalds, and Russell Bakers who might—if they keep up their efforts—make us realize how fatuous we have become.

Chapter 6

INFLATION AND ITS CAUSES

Stagflation

Americans have experienced a growing feeling of helplessness and frustration as they have watched prices spiral upward. Economists don't agree on the causes of inflation, so they can't agree on what ought to be done about it. They are not themselves in a position to do anything about inflation or, for that matter, any other economic problem. All they can do is offer advice. But are economists just as baffled by inflation as everyone else? The answer, alas, is "no." The problem is not that economists don't understand inflation. It's that neither they nor elected officials can agree on a program that would stabilize prices.

One sure way to bring inflation to a screeching halt—and to maintain price stability—would be to impose comprehensive, mandatory wage and price controls. Any competent economist could design a system of controls—including rollbacks where necessary—which would prevent further price increases. So why don't our lawmakers ask them to do this? Controls worked well during World War II. But under peacetime conditions most politicians seem to find the idea of wage and price controls to be morally offensive.

Public opinion polls have shown that a majority of citizens would vote for such controls. Those on fixed incomes, many workers who have seen their purchasing power eroded during the past ten years, and committed "liberals" who believe in the beneficence of government, would cheerfully accept rationing and the other inconveniences of a price-controlled economy—if the alternative is to be further steady erosion of the American standard of living by inflation. Controls, in spite of the problems involved in administering them, contain an element of "fairness" in the distribution of what is available.

Everyone doesn't suffer from inflation. Many business and professional persons, investors, federal government employees, and even some hourly workers in the private sector are able to keep abreast or ahead of inflation. They keep the market for luxury goods and recreation booming, and they would assail any proposal for comprehensive wage and price controls as an attack on the American way of life. There really isn't much point in talking about mandatory wage and price controls. Even if conditions got much worse, the probability that comprehensive controls would be proposed in Congress is exceedingly small. The "new conservatives" of the Reagan administration want to diminish the amount of governmental involvement in the economy, not add to it.

Isn't there some middle way? Is the choice one of a free market versus comprehensive controls? Couldn't the government ask unions to stop pressing for wage increases? Can't businesses be urged to limit price increases to those specified by "non-inflationary" guidelines?

The trouble with partial measures is that they have been tried, and they haven't worked. A number of economists involved in Nixon's wage and price stabilization program have written books about their experiences. Most admit the failure of voluntary wage and price guidelines. Surprisingly, some conclude that while voluntary stabilization programs have failed they are the only hope for the future. The logic of that argument is hard to follow.

The problem is that conventional economics—whether it focuses on demand or production stimuli—still guides the thinking of policymakers. And politicians will continue to tinker with tax cuts and the money supply, hoping thus to stimulate employment and retard inflation. But conventional monetary and fiscal policies haven't worked for years—why should they work now? The rate of inflation will vary from time to time as it is influenced by external forces such as the 1981 "oil glut." But the long-run, rising trend will continue unabated. That doesn't mean the American economy is on the verge of collapse. It built up enormous layers of economic fat during the years of rapid growth. Slow erosion of the standard of living can go on for a long time without genuinely disastrous consequences. Meanwhile, various groups and organizations will continue to point the finger of blame at one another. Each, of course, considers the others to be the cause of inflation.

Corporations and Inflation

Are large corporations a major cause of inflation? Some economists think so. Robert Lekachman, one of the group of economists who have dubbed themselves "post-Keynesians," argued in the *New Republic* of October 14, 1978, that major corporations aren't responsive to market forces. They raise prices even when the demand for their products is falling. This is not a new discovery; it's a point J. K. Galbraith has been making for years. But Lekachman implies that such behavior is contradictory to the postulates of conventional economics.

There is, in fact, nothing contradictory about such behavior, and that would be true even in a perfectly competitive market. It would be a contradiction only if one assumed that everything else in the economy remained unchanged. But if the costs of labor, materials, energy, transportation, and so on, go up—as they do under conditions of general inflation—it's not only possible but certain that corporations will raise prices. If they would do this in competitive markets, it surely should surprise no one that corporations behave as they do when they buy and sell in markets that aren't price-competitive.

Conventional economics recognizes that some markets are monopolistic rather than competitive. By "monopoly" traditional economists mean a single seller of a product (or service) for which there is no close substitute. Few examples of pure monopoly can be found. Instead, we observe "oligopoly"—or markets dominated by a few large sellers. Examples are the steel, auto, aluminum, aircraft, oil, and many other major manufacturing industries.

Lekachman believes that oligopolies behave like monopolies. They restrict output to raise prices. The only difference is that they compete actively via advertising, but advertising adds to the prices consumers have to pay. Not all economists agree. J. K. Galbraith—another post-Keynesian—has argued that large companies enjoy economies of experience and scale. The gains from these economies could more than offset the cost of advertising. High as the prices of automobiles are today, for instance, they are lower than they would be if cars were manufactured in thousands of small competitive shops.

Lekachman picked an inappropriate example of the inflationary effects of an oligopoly when he chose the oil industry. No one seriously believes that the Seven Sisters engage in aggressive price competition. But if they have been in collusion—tacit or otherwise—to do anything, it has been to keep U.S. petroleum consumption up and prices down. How else can one explain the relatively low gasoline prices in this country? In Europe and Latin America, excluding Mexico, gasoline prices are two to three times as high as the U.S. average. In the U.S. gasoline remains an unalloyed bargain.

Cheap gasoline can't last. Within the coming decade gasoline prices will rise faster than other prices. Even the oil companies won't be able to hold them down once the oil "glut" of the early 1980s is replaced by the "gap" which energy experts project before 1990. The increases in gasoline prices which followed the major oil price hikes after 1978 resulted in a modest drop in consumption. As prices continue to increase, consumers will back off still more. But these changes will be the result of actual scarcity, not collusion.

Economists who believe that the pricing practices of large corporations are inflationary also feel that this would simplify the problem of imposing controls. We don't need controls across the board, they maintain, only on a few hundred large corporations. It's a delusion, however, to think such controls would work. In a limited way Nixon's price controllers tried that approach. It failed abysmally. The problem of selective controls is illustrated by the case of chicken broilers. The price of chicken feed wasn't limited, but ceiling prices were imposed on broilers. Producers faced with rising production costs, and ceilings on their prices, responded by killing thousands of embryonic broilers.

Those who would impose selective controls fail to recognize a fundamental characteristic of a modern economy—that is, its interdependence. The intricate network of suppliers and buyers—all dependent on one another—insures the failure of any system of partial controls.

Does this mean we're at the mercy of Big Business? Actually, no. The case against large corporations as a major cause of inflation hasn't been proved. There has been little change in the pattern of industrial concentration over the past quarter century. Yet during this time there have been some periods, such as 1960–65, when prices were relatively stable and real income rose. If corporations cause inflation now, why not then?

None of this should be construed as an apology for large corporations. They have undue political influence, and given the chance will behave rapaciously in the marketplace. But the behavior of corporations is restrained in a number of ways—by government, by unions, and even on rare occasions by consumers who have been pushed too far. Witness the spontaneous switch from American to foreign automobiles when American manufacturers failed to adjust to the reality of rising gasoline prices, and in many cases failed to match the quality of their competitors' products.

In fairness, one has to point out that Lekachman doesn't regard partial price controls as a panacea. That is good, since there's little chance they will be adopted. Partial controls would do nothing to alleviate the problems of slow growth, declining productivity, and growing scarcities, which are the root causes of inflation.

If lawmakers were serious about restraining inflation, they would turn to comprehensive controls and an equitable system of rationing. The alternative is further tinkering with monetary and fiscal policies, which might retard price increases slightly in the short term, but which almost certainly would depress the already slow growth rate. That could contribute to long-term inflationary pressures and the additional inequities which continued inflation will beget.

Unions and Inflation

I once conducted a small, completely unscientific poll by asking a half-dozen friends—none of whom belongs to a union—if they thought trade unions are inflationary. The uniform response was a look of surprise and a quick "Of course!" A couple countered with the question "Don't you?" When I replied "I don't know," there were more surprised looks. Economists are supposed to know such things.

Some of the nation's more eminent economic practitioners—ranging from the ultra-conservative Milton Friedman to the liberal Kenneth Boulding—have argued that unions can't have a lasting effect on wages. Wages, they claim, "are determined by marginal productivity." If an employer were to hire workers one at a time, to perform identical jobs, he could record the amount each added to the company's total output. The output added by the last worker hired is labor's "marginal product" in that company.

The price which the company in this illustration charges for whatever it makes, we have to assume, is set by a free market. The company has no control over price; it is a "price-taker." Similarly, this theory assumes, wages are determined by the demand for and supply of each occupation or other "pool" of labor. Neither the employer nor anyone else has actual control over wages.

Everyone knows that unions negotiate wage rates in many industries. But marginal productivity theorists believe that the negotiated rates are the same as those that would be determined by a smoothly operating free market. The classic statement of this position—greatly oversimplified here because of space limitations—was given by Nobel laureate Sir John Hicks in his book *The Theory of Wages* (Macmillan, 1932).

Since the employer knows the value of labor's marginal product, he will hire workers until this value equals the market-determined wage rate. At that point his company is "in equilibrium." If the company isn't in equilibrium, it isn't "maximizing profits." And maximizing profits, traditional economic theory tells us, is what business is all about.

Not all economists accept this view. Many believe that unions do have a major impact on prices because they view them as monopolies, and monopolies, by definition, raise prices by restricting supply. If a monopoly doesn't restrict output and raise prices, it isn't "maximizing profits." A union monopoly, we are told, will try to maximize wages.

One has to point out, in fairness, that not all economists who think that unions are monopolistic are "union busters." Some realize that unions are necessary to protect workers from exploitation by large corporations. Those who feel that unions raise wages above "competitive" levels usually believe that corporations raise prices above "competitive" levels. A prescription some have offered is that big companies be divided into small, competing units. Collective bargaining would then be limited to these smaller companies and local unions. This, some traditional economists believe, would take the nation a step closer to the competitive model which the followers of Adam Smith said would result in "the best of all possible worlds."

It's clear that arguments such as the above influence policy makers. The results, unfortunately, don't always follow the reasoning given in textbooks. President Carter, for example, stressed the need for more competition. He appointed Alfred Kahn, former chairman of the Civil Aeronautics Board, as his wage-price czar. Kahn had come to his new job fresh from a victorious battle to "deregulate" the airlines. Unfortunately, deregulation didn't produce the results promised by the textbooks which Kahn evidently took at face value. Instead of lower prices, air fares went up. Instead of better service, many smaller communities lost major airline connections. Airline "competition," in brief, was anything but the great boon which Alfred Kahn and his supporters said it would be.

Some economists have difficulty with the arguments outlined earlier. These stem from skepticism about the usefulness of conventional "neoclassical economics"—the dominant academic school of thought today. Neoclassical studies are attractive, logical games. But they oversimplify to the point that few are relevant to the problems of the real world.

There is also less than a universal desire for more competition. What most people want, actually, is for everyone else to be more competitive. Competition might be great if everyone would compete, but if some compete and some don't, the result is anything but "the best of all possible worlds." In the days of aggressive price competition in coal, for instance, some operators made fortunes; other failed. Cheap coal helped industrialize urban America. But it did nothing for the miners, whose wages were depressed by competition, and it did nothing for the coal-producing regions which bore the social costs of coal extraction while distant industrial cities reaped the benefits.

When we're in an inflationary spiral, no one really knows whether wages chase prices or prices chase wages. Also, collective bargaining goes on when we have inflation and when we don't. It would be a lot easier to work out cause and effect relationships—and to pin the blame for inflation on the guilty party or parties—if most of the things that are blamed for inflation today hadn't been around in the fondly remembered days of relative price stability. Unions were stronger, in a relative sense, during the early 1960s—when prices were stable—than they are now. Again, if unions "cause" inflation now, why didn't they cause it then?

Deficit Spending: The *Causa Causans* of Inflation

Politicians trying to unseat incumbents ride the inflation issue with unabated fervor. Some voters, driven to desperation by the upward spiral of prices, gamble on them. After all, they must reason, what is there to lose? The incumbents haven't held prices down. Maybe their challengers will. Ronald Reagan's campaign certainly was helped by inflation.

Challengers inevitably maintain that we have to get down to basics, and the first of these is a balanced budget. Deficit spending, they say, is the root cause of inflation. It is an evil that must be extirpated if the dollar is to be protected from further erosion.

If deficit spending is the primary cause of inflation, as some maintain, an increase in the deficit should be followed by accelerated price increases. Conversely, if the deficit drops, consumer prices should level off.

Table 4 compares changes in the consumer price index with changes in the federal deficit. The early years, 1962–65, represent a period of relative price stability. Since 1974 we have had moderate to severe inflation.

The deficit more than doubled in 1962. But the price index went up only 1.1 percent. The next year the deficit dropped by one-third, but prices rose 1.2 percent. A larger deficit saw only a slight increase in prices in 1964. But a drastic drop in the deficit in 1964—when we almost had a balanced budget—was accompanied by the biggest price increase of the early period.

Table 4

**Percent Changes in the Consumer Price Index and
the Federal Budget Deficit**

Year	Consumer Price Index	Fed. Budget Deficit
1962	+ 1.1%	+109.5%
1963	+ 1.2	− 33.4
1964	+ 1.3	+ 24.6
1965	+ 1.7	− 73.0
1974	+11.0	− 68.4
1975	+ 9.1	+861.9
1976	+ 5.8	+ 47.3
1977	+ 6.5	− 32.2
1978	+ 7.7	+ 8.6
1979	+11.3	− 43.2
1980	+13.5	+115.1

Source: *Economic Report of the President, 1981.*

In more recent years, the deficit dropped by two-thirds between 1973 and 1974. That year consumer prices rose 11 percent. It was the most inflationary year until 1979. A ninefold increase in the deficit in 1975 reflected the quadrupling of oil and coal prices the year before, but the price index rose at a slower rate. A further increase in the deficit the next year was accompanied by a modest price rise. There was a large jump in prices in 1979, but the deficit dropped 43 percent that year. Both prices and the deficit moved up sharply in 1980.

Large changes in deficits had little effect on prices in the early 1960s. In recent years prices have risen whether the deficit went up or down. For the entire period the statistical relationship is extremely weak, with a correlation coefficient of 0.04. This is about as close as one can get to no correlation at all. The federal deficit would be a poor predictor of price increases, and vice versa. This was illustrated by events during the first quarter of 1982. The Reagan administration's projected budgets included deficits of almost $99 billion for 1982, $91 billion for 1983, and $83 billion for 1984. Still, the rate of inflation dropped steadily during the first quarter of 1982. In April there was an absolute decline in the consumer price index, the first in eight years.

The results of an interesting study of deficits and inflation were reported in the October 5, 1981, edition of the *Wall Street Journal.* It was a cross-sectional, international study made by Alan Reynolds, vice-president of Polyeconomics, Inc. It is worth noting that this company is a consulting firm representing the highly conservative "supply-side" stance discussed briefly in Chapter 2.

Reynolds found, for example, that Colombia had a modest budget *surplus* of 5.5 percent in 1977–79, but its consumer prices went up more than 25 percent between 1977 and 1980. Japan, on the other hand, had a large deficit of 32 percent. Its consumer prices rose only 5.9 percent. Brazil, with a miniscule deficit of 3.2 percent, had the highest inflation rate—almost 55 percent—among the fourteen countries Reynolds studied.

In spite of abundant evidence to the contrary, a number of economic commentators continue to preach the doctrine that the fundamental cause of inflation is the federal budget deficit. Although one should regard such claims with skepticism, it doesn't follow that budget deficits have nothing to do with inflation. Both the consumer price index and the deficit are affected by numerous forces. It is necessary to consider all of them when attempting to identify the manifold causes of inflation.

A balanced budget also doesn't necessarily indicate that all's right with the economy. The U.S. has had a balanced budget eight times in the last thirty-one years; each time there was a recession. Reduced revenues and rising unemployment inevitably brought back deficits. Deficits themselves aren't the problem, although the size of the deficit is critically important.

What bothers most individuals about deficits is the knowledge that they themselves can't go ever deeper into debt without courting economic disaster. So how can the government do it? There are two reasons. First, unlike individuals, the government has "perpetual life." It doesn't have to worry about "settling an estate" at the end of some normal life span. Second, it can influence the debt by manipulating the money supply.

When will the government pay off its ever-mounting debt? Probably never. What matters, however, are the rates at which national output and debt grow. If output grows faster than debt, the "burden" of the debt is declining and deficits tend to shrink in real terms. When the reverse is true, the economy is in trouble. Like a thermometer which signals illness by registering a high temperature, a rising deficit tells us we should be looking for the basic causes of our economic distress.

Balancing the Federal Budget

The idea that a balanced federal budget is desirable is a vintage illusion believed by those unable to differentiate between a household and that complicated entity we call "the government." The idea of a constitutional amendment requiring the federal budget to be balanced every year—or even over a period of several years—makes no economic sense. This is a time of strange political undercurrents, however, and sensible or not, such a requirement could become law.

The balanced-budget "movement" is another manifestation of public concern about inflation. Voters disturbed by declining real income are responsive to any promise of relief from further price increases. It has become an article of faith that budget deficits are a primary cause of inflation. This belief persists in spite of evidence such as that given in the preceding section. The sad fact is that if the balanced-budget amendment were adopted it would have little or no effect on prices. There probably also would be no real change in the federal government's fiscal behavior. The balanced-budget drive is built on illusions.

Many individuals feel that since they have to balance their budgets the federal government should do likewise. But there's an important difference between individuals and their government. An individual can't continuously borrow money to pay off old debts without courting disaster. The federal government, however, does this regularly. The federal debt is constantly recycled. The government sells securities to raise money for the retirement of securities that have become due. It can do this because, in principle, it has "perpetual life." The government doesn't have to worry about the threat of bankruptcy as it recycles debt.

Does this mean there are no limits on the amounts the government can borrow? Obviously not. A limit is established by the "burden" of the debt. Individuals and businesses who lend money to the federal government expect to receive interest. The total burden of the public debt is measured by the interest component of the federal budget. If this component increased faster than the Gross National Product for a period of years, there would be cause for concern. Up to now this hasn't happened.

The federal deficit could be eliminated by the stroke of a pen if government were to adopt the accounting conventions of private business. When a private corporation buys a new building, for example, the value of that building is carried on its books as an asset. The amount paid for the building is, of course, a liability. When the federal government spends a billion dollars to construct new highways, however, only the expenditure is reported. Nowhere is this addition to the nation's assets, or wealth, accounted for. Unlike private businesses, government books do not include a capital account.

The lack of capital accounting in the federal budget is not an oversight. It's difficult to establish a price for most of the things the government builds. Markets determine the prices of things that businesses buy and sell, and those prices determine the value of their acquired assets. The federal government could, however, consider the cost of constructing any facility as the asset value of that facility. Alternatively, during an inflationary period, it could estimate the replacement cost of existing assets. In one way or another the government could add a capital account to those it presently keeps. Such an account would almost certainly wipe out even the relatively large deficits of recent years. For most years, in fact, the federal budget would show a healthy surplus. A change in accounting methods would be the most likely response to a constitutional amendment requiring balanced budgets.

The time and effort going into the balanced-budget movement are misdirected. Instead of trying to impose an unworkable fiscal straitjacket on the federal government, balanced-budget advocates should focus on the elimination of waste, duplication, and inefficiency in government. Public jobs should not be regarded as sinecures. Those paid from public funds—whether at the federal, state, or local levels—should be held as accountable as anyone working for a private firm.

The lamentable feature of movements which seek a painless nostrum for inflation is that they divert attention from the only workable solution—comprehensive, mandatory price and wage controls. Controls would, of course, create a new set of problems; but if policy makers are serious about limiting inflation, these problems could be handled. Whatever else might be said about controls, they would result in a more equitable distribution of what we produce than any proposal advanced to date. They would certainly produce a more evenhanded distribution than we will see if inflation is allowed to continue unabated.

Hedging Against Inflation

Many Americans apparently believe that inflation is here to stay. The question, then, is how to beat it. The answer, unhappily, is that most of us won't. Erosion of the standard of living of a wide cross-section of American society is likely to continue.

Investors saving for retirement or for the future education of their children are shifting out of security markets into tangible assets—

many into real estate. This has been encouraged by the internal revenue code, which gives property owners a once-for-all exemption of $125,000 capital gain on the sale of residential property occupied by the owner or owners. That should comfortably get one or more children through college. But what then?

Relatively young couples, especially where both are working, are "trading up" their houses. A moderately priced house bought ten years ago for a small down payment often sells for more than twice its original price. This provides the down payment on a more expensive dwelling. In a few years—assuming real estate prices continue to escalate—the process can be repeated. The couple might have little in the way of liquid assets, but their net worth will climb steadily. For some in the right age bracket (young enough to get mortgages), this has been one way to beat inflation. But there's no guarantee—in this world of compounding uncertainties—that it's foolproof.

The marketplace has a way of punishing latecomers to the game of speculation. If enough homeowners try to hedge against inflation by trading up, the bubble could burst at some point. The age distribution of the population is changing. The baby boom, which started at the end of World War II and continued until the mid-1960s, has come to an end. Between 1964 and 1977, the number of persons under five declined by 5 million, or 26 percent. The new "thin generation" has already caused school and college enrollments to drop; its members will be entering the labor force—and the housing market—in diminishing numbers during the 1980s.

It would be fatuous to try to pinpoint a time when the upward spiral of housing prices might end. But speculative buying is pushing housing prices up at an alarming rate in some parts of the country. A good illustration of the effects of overzealous speculation was provided a few years ago when condominium apartments were vastly overbuilt in Ocean City, Maryland. When the first few buildings were finished, apartments were snapped up by buyers who wanted vacation property that could pay part of its way by rental income when not used by the owners.

The basic idea is a sound one, provided there is enough demand to clear the market of new units as they become available. But the initial demand was so strong that it attracted speculators from far and wide. They bought apartments with minimal down payments and resold them as soon as possible at higher prices. Some of the buyers were other speculators who turned them over at still higher prices. But such wild escalation can't last. Successful speculators are cagey enough to know when to unload. Enough of them knew when to pull out in the Ocean City case, and, after they did, the market collapsed.

Many of the newer condominiums went into receivership. The banks that had financed them were anxious to cut their losses, and apartment prices fell sharply. In a few years the market stabilized, and this experience isn't likely to be repeated in that particular area. Some of the banks involved sustained considerable losses, including a few of New York's major lending agencies. But individuals who had bought apartments at highly inflated prices also suffered losses.

No one would seriously suggest a nationwide collapse in the housing market at the present time. There has been, in fact, a growing gap between the formation of new households and the construction of new units. This has maintained upward pressure on resale prices, especially in growing communities. The moral of the Ocean City saga is that speculative buying *can* cause markets to collapse in specific areas. Buyers of real estate in such areas could have their savings wiped out. That would be even worse, of course, than watching the purchasing power of one's financial assets diminish gradually year by year.

The sad fact is that there is no general-purpose hedge against inflation. Those with wealth aren't troubled. They, or their financial managers, can shift investments around—and maintain enough diversity—to ensure that their assets hold or increase their value, while the income stream from them continues to rise as prices go up. But one needs a lot of money to play that game successfully. Most of us don't have the entry fee.

Some optimists argue that inflation can't last much longer. But they don't say why. A number of countries—Great Britain, for example—have had more severe inflation than the U.S. for a longer time without revolutionary political consequences. Since our political leaders lack the understanding—or the courage—to stop inflation by the only method that is guaranteed to work, namely, mandatory, comprehensive price and wage controls, it's a fairly safe guess that like the British we will muddle through. For most of us this will mean still further losses in asset values, and further declines in real income.

Inflation and Depressions

The suggestion that the nation can survive an indefinite period of inflation will not be convincing to those who are convinced the U.S. economy is on a collision course with disaster. The inevitable dénouement of serious inflation, they believe, is a severe depression. What are the chances that they're right?

The difference between a recession and a depression is the difference between a severe cold and cancer. Colds are a common occurrence; even the healthiest persons have colds. Cancer, however, means a serious organic breakdown. Unless all diseased cells are extirpated, the patient will die.

We've only had one depression in the U.S. during this century. It started with the stock market crash of October 1929 and ended eleven years later. Events leading to depressions build up slowly; they don't happen overnight. The crash of 1929 was the final link in a causal chain which started with overexpansion of farm capacity during World War I. Throughout the 1920s industry boomed. Farmers tried to cope with falling prices by expanding production. This only added to excess farm capacity and still lower prices. Since food prices dropped during the 1920s, industrial paychecks were stretched without wage increases. Unions had gained a small toehold during World War I but lost ground during the roaring twenties. There was virtually no regulation of business and finance. Speculators had a free hand. Lured by the promise of a "car in every garage, and a chicken in every pot," small savers surrendered their funds. After the crash they didn't have a pot to put a chicken in—even if they were lucky enough to find the chicken.

The American economy got completely out of balance during the 1920s. That decade marked the apogee of unrestrained "free enterprise." When economic power is not accompanied by responsibility and accountability, the system is without checks and balances. There was no Security and Exchange Commission to puncture the inflated claims of speculators. Employers didn't have to recognize unions, so wages were determined by management fiat. There were no Social Security or unemployment payments to help the aged and the jobless. The system was lopsided and unstable. The superficial prosperity of the 1920s was built on a crumbling foundation.

Most economists were confused by the Great Depression. Free markets were supposed to maintain "equilibrium," but the market system broke down in 1929. In 1936 John Maynard Keynes published his correct diagnosis of the problem as a lack of effective demand. By "effective demand" Keynes meant the demand for investment goods— or what economists call "capital"—and the demand for consumer goods. His prescription was to bolster effective demand by stimulating investment and by government action to expand consumer spending. Both were to be accomplished by appropriate monetary and fiscal policies.

World War II showed that Keynes's diagnosis was correct. Unemployment virtually disappeared, and the nation's industrial capacity grew to meet the skyrocketing demand for military and civilian goods. Meanwhile, Social Security and unemployment insurance funds were building. Unions made monumental strides in organizing industry. By the end of the war, the American economy had been transformed.

The new system of modified capitalism didn't eliminate recessions. They continued to occur more or less regularly, but there are now too many "built-in stabilizers" for recessions to degenerate into another depression. When production slows because of a lack of demand, workers are laid off. They collect unemployment compensation, so consumer spending doesn't fall as fast as production. Social Security, veterans' benefits, and other "transfer payments" help sustain consumer spending. The likelihood of a depression under these conditions is miniscule. The probability of a recession, however, is high. It will result from weak and ineffective efforts to stem inflation. Recent anti-inflation programs haven't had much effect on prices.

There's a far more serious threat than the possibility of depression which traditional economists—including those in government—

haven't faced up to. This is the major slowdown in long-term economic growth since 1969. Past recessions occurred around a rising growth trend. Now that trend line is almost horizontal.

The Great Depression was caused by inadequate demand. Today's growth difficulties stem from the supply side—from sharply increasing energy prices, and resource scarcities which cause sharp price increases. The result is a new kind of inflation which doesn't respond to monetary and fiscal measures.

The "supply-side" economists are aware that policies designed to stimulate demand aren't the answer to inflation. Their proposals for increasing the supply of goods and services—by increasing the inducement to invest and reducing the amount of government regulation—also fail to get at the heart of the problem engendered by rising *real* energy and resource costs. These, in turn, have adversely affected productivity, and rising productivity was the prime mover of robust economic growth, both here and abroad, during the 1960s. We'll return to this important issue later in this chapter. But there are other matters relating to inflation which should be cleared up first.

There was considerable discussion, early in 1980, about the reliability of the U.S. Department of Labor's Consumer Price Index (CPI), the economic indicator which is used to estimate the rate of inflation. At issue was the CPI's housing component which had been rising very rapidly. That, of course, pulled up the whole index. But most of us don't buy a house every month, so some economists argued that the housing component gave the index an "upward bias." In the words of a leading business journal: "We're better off than we think."

The Anatomy of Inflation

Anyone fortunate enough to have taken out a long-term, low-interest mortgage many years ago isn't affected by current increases in the prices of new homes or the record-high interest rates of the early 1980s. There's more to the housing component of the CPI, however, than the cost of new houses. It also covers the cost of maintenance and improvements. And the latter component applies to all of us, owners and renters alike. Perhaps the only way to deal with the problem would be to have two indexes, one for those who buy new houses and one for those who don't.

The latter suggestion, which is entirely facetious, raises a question of genuine significance; namely, whose cost of living does the CPI measure? The correct answer is—no one's. This may startle readers aware that many labor management agreements contain cost-of-living adjustments, and that the CPI affects the take-home pay of federal employees and other workers, organized and unorganized. But it's easy to demonstrate that this is the correct answer.

The CPI isn't a bureaucratic gimmick designed to fool the public or provide backdoor favors to union leaders. It represents the best efforts of competent statisticians to estimate the effects of price changes on a so-called typical or average urban family of four. Each month the Bureau of Labor Statistics (BLS) collects price information about a market basket of goods and services which the hypothetical family purchases.

At present, sample surveys are conducted in eighty-five urban areas which include about 80 percent of the country's population. The BLS has been conducting these surveys periodically since February 1921. Major revisions have been made from time to time to keep the index up-to-date. The latest revision was started in 1970 and finished in 1978—at a cost of $50 million. Good statistical work takes time, and it can't be done on a shoestring budget. Even then, the result is a very imperfect instrument for the measurement of inflation.

This should not be construed as criticism of the BLS statisticians. The top people in this agency are well known and highly regarded in scholarly and scientific circles. There are some things, however, that can't be measured with precision; inflation is one of them. But the BLS strives to give us the best estimates it can.

Prices are collected on scores of commodities and services classified into eight broad categories. These categories, and the weights used in the last two revisions of the CPI, are given in Table 5.

The controversial component—housing—is subdivided into rent, home purchase, financing, taxes, insurance, maintenance and repairs, fuel oil, coal, gas, electricity, house furnishings, house supplies, and

Table 5

**Percentage of Income Expended
On Commodities and Services**

Expenditure Group	Year 1962	Year 1972-73
Food and alcoholic beverages	25.2	20.4
Housing	34.9	39.8
Apparel	10.6	7.0
Transportation	14.0	19.8
Medical care	5.7	4.2
Entertainment	3.9	4.3
Personal care	2.8	1.8
Other goods and services	2.9	2.7

Source: U.S. Department of Labor, Bureau of Labor Statistics.

household services. Every consumer doesn't make all of these payments each month. Renters probably pay only fuel and electricity costs in addition to rent. Homeowners, however, make a number of the other payments. An individual might be interested in comparing Table 5 with his or her family budget using the 1972-73 market basket. That is one way to tell how close the national CPI comes to estimating changes in the cost of living in a specific household.

The BLS publishes information about the price changes that have the greatest influence on its index in monthly news releases. If an individual followed those releases—and kept a record of monthly expenditures—that person would have a general idea of how he or she was affected by inflation compared with the bureau's hypothetical urban family. Because of the enormous diversity of the U.S. economy, there is no single index that can mean much to a specific household. The CPI remains the best general indicator of price changes in the United States. What we all have to realize is that it provides estimates only.

There are numerous problems in addition to the housing issue that plague index makers. One is the perennial issue of quality change. Some critics of the CPI say it has an "upward bias" because it fails to show that new products are superior to old products. But no one has been able to demonstrate that all quality changes represent improvement. It wouldn't be hard to compile a list of products—and services—showing quality deterioration. The CPI might cancel these positive and negative changes as well as any other index.

A Do-It-Yourself Price Index

Trying to figure out who is hurt most by inflation might be a problem without a solution. The *Wall Street Journal*, of January 8, 1980, reported that ten economists and a sociologist had been questioned about the matter. Eleven different answers were given.

Two economists discussed inflation's "transfer effect." One stated that the young gain at the expense of the old—particularly the elderly who saved for retirement. Many young persons are going into debt to pay for an education, or to buy houses at inflated prices. Those who borrow to continue their education hope, of course, that their earning power will be enhanced. But whatever happens, they'll pay their debts in cheaper dollars. Similarly, young house buyers are likely to gain, assuming they are able to overcome the hurdles of large down payments and high interest rates. First, they're acquiring assets that should increase in value as inflation persists. Borrowers able to arrange long-term mortgages—even at high interest rates—will pay them off in progressively cheaper dollars. And a substantial part of their interest payments will be tax deductible.

There is no guarantee that housing prices will continue to escalate as they have. Temporary and localized setbacks in housing markets aren't likely, however, to eliminate all the gains from inflation. And a general housing "bust" is no more imminent than a general depression.

Another respondent mentioned a different transfer effect. Some self-employed persons—doctors, appliance repairmen, plumbers, and the like—can increase their service charges faster than other prices rise. Those who are entirely dependent on wages and salaries can't do this.

So there's a transfer of income from the "employed" to the "self-employed." This can happen only where the demand for the services of the self-employed is greater than the available supply, but that situation seems fairly common.

Only one respondent pointed out that the CPI "doesn't apply to anybody." Yet union members covered by cost-of-living adjustments, federal employees (including retirees), and Social Security recipients receive wage or pension increases as this index goes up. No one knows whether the cost of living is going up as fast, or faster than, the incomes of those workers and retirees. Some individuals or households are no doubt losing ground while others gain. It depends on the location of the individual or household and on their consumption habits. It also depends on a host of other variables, and we probably don't know what all of them are.

One way an individual can tell whether he or she is keeping up with the cost of living is to construct a "tailor-made" index. This isn't difficult provided expenditures have been recorded or can be estimated closely. It's always possible, of course, to start keeping a record now and to make the first year with complete records a personal "base year." Use the eight expenditure categories given above—the ones used by the Bureau of Labor Statistics.

Record the distribution of *after-tax* income under each of the categories (state and federal taxes aren't included in the Cost-of-Living Index—property taxes are). The percentage distribution of expenditures will be the index "weights." Record expenditures monthly. At the end of the year set up a table for the eight categories like Table 6.

The expenditures times their weights are called "cross products." These are added for both years. The base year total is divided into the same total for the next year. In the above example, divide 34,405 by 32,300. The result is a 7 percent increase. If this hypothetical individual's after-tax income had gone up 8 percent, he or she would have been ahead of inflation. If it had gone up less, this person would have fallen behind.

Notice that the weights in this simple index don't change. They should remain constant as long as the same base year is used. One might want to update periodically a personal index by selecting a new

Table 6

Sample Individualized Consumer Price Index

Expenditure Category	Base Year			Next Year		
	Expen- ditures	Weights	Cross Product	Expen- ditures	Weights	Cross Product
A	$200	× 22% =	4,400	$250	× 22% =	5,500
B	$300	× 33% =	9,900	$310	× 33% =	10,230
C	$400	× 45% =	18,000	$415	× 45% =	18,675
Total	$900	× 100% =	32,300	$975	× 100% =	34,405

base year and calculating a new set of weights. Making and updating such an index requires some effort, but it could be worth it. It would let the person willing to make this effort know where he or she stands in the "great inflation exchange."

One respondent to the *Wall Street Journal's* survey said: Inflation is one of the great democratic institutions. . . . It hits everybody." This isn't entirely so. It doesn't hit everyone in the same way, or to the same extent. Some gain, some lose. The only way you as an individual will know how inflation affects you is to compare changes in your income with changes in the prices of the goods and services you buy—not with a statistical indicator that is useful for some purposes, but which doesn't measure any specific person's cost of living.

Productivity

Corporations, unions, and federal budget deficits have been identified by different groups as the major causes of inflation. But the discussion in preceding sections raises a question about these charges. If they are the causes today, why didn't they cause inflation during the 1960s? Neither unions nor corporations are stronger today than they were then. And the statistical relationship between changes in the budget deficit and changes in prices isn't remotely close. So what has changed since the nation last experienced stable prices? Two things stand out:

(1) a declining rate of economic growth and (2) declining productivity. The two go hand in hand.

An economy "grows" when it produces goods and services at a faster rate than its population growth rate. Rising productivity is thus a necessary condition for robust economic growth. Indexes of productivity show changes in economic efficiency from a base year and may be expressed per worker or in worker-hours. Productivity indexes measure changes in the efficiency of the *entire system*, however, not only changes in worker effort or ability.

Table 7 shows what has happened to productivity in the U.S. The early years represent a five-year period of stable prices; the later years cover an inflationary period of equal length.

Table 7

Changes in Productivity

	Percent Changes	
	1960-65	*1975–80*
Real GNP Per Worker	16.3	4.6
Output Per Worker-Hour	21.3	4.9

Source: Calculated from data in *Economic Report of the President, 1981.*

Table 7 shows that there has been a precipitous decline in productivity. How do changes in productivity affect prices? Prices are determined by demand and supply. In the U.S., however, after World War II, federal officials tried to deal with economic problems by manipulating demand. Supply, they assumed, would take care of itself. When the major concern was unemployment, the federal government stimulated demand by encouraging borrowing. When inflation became the dominant problem, it discouraged demand by increasing interest rates and restricting credit. Neither policy worked well after the late 1960s. Since then, unemployment and inflation have coexisted. This is one of the consequences of declining productivity and economic growth.

Declining growth rates create a situation that traditional economists—and those they advise—haven't yet learned to deal with. If the rate at which we produce goods and provide services slows down, while the money supply doesn't, there can be only one result—inflation.

Why is the economy growing so slowly? First, it's partly a victim of its own success. By the 1960s we had become adept at producing things. But when we added to the growing stock of production facilities and goods, we also filled the air and water with pollutants and littered the landscape with solid waste. The reaction was a series of environmental laws. No thoughtful person will question the desirability of clean air and clean water legislation. We have to recognize, however, that they add to production costs without increasing productivity. As the early textbooks on environmental economics pointed out, there's no such thing as a free lunch. If we want a clean environment—as those do who can afford it—the nation must pay for it in part by a slower growth rate.

Health and safety legislation also have had adverse effects on productivity. Society shouldn't expect coal miners and industrial workers to pay a high price in lives lost and bodies maimed so that the rest of us can have a higher standard of living; but when work places are made safer and less deleterious to health, productivity falls. High productivity and industrial safety are both desirable objectives, but we have had to trade some losses in productivity for gains in industrial safety.

Another cause of declining productivity is the ancient law of diminishing returns, which is inexorable and irreversible. As we use up the world's finite supplies of resources and energy, additional units cost more to discover, extract, process, and consume. The additional time, effort, and equipment to add to production result in declining output per worker. More will be said about diminishing returns and productivity later.

Until the nation's political leaders recognize that the causes of our economic problems are interdependent, there will be no basic change in policy. Although the Reagan administration professed to attack economic problems from the supply side, it has done so using conventional fiscal weapons. These are not likely to be any more effective in stimulating production and productivity than they have been in reducing unemployment and inflation.

Production and Productivity

The terms "productivity" and "production" are sometimes confused, but they have totally different meanings. Production simply means output; it refers to tons of coal, tons of steel, numbers of automobiles, and so forth. Production also includes services provided—pupils taught, haircuts given, babies delivered, and the like. Statisticians estimate the total quantity of goods and services produced in a given time period. The result is called Gross National Product (GNP). The rate at which GNP is changing is one of the more widely used indicators of the health of the economy.

Productivity is a more complicated idea. It is derived from the notion of "efficiency." Economists estimate changes in productivity by dividing changes in output by changes in a single input—labor time— rather than by changes in all of the inputs used in the production process. Thus, we see frequent references to "labor productivity," but this is a misnomer. If we were, in fact, measuring labor time and labor effort only—with all other inputs held constant—a productivity index would measure changes in labor productivity. What the index actually measures, however, is the change in output due to changes in all inputs. It is only expressed in units of labor time. It could just as easily be expressed in Btus.

Productivity is reported in labor time because the latter is easily measured, but it takes other resources—and capital equipment—to produce anything. A man digging coal with a pick and shovel is using little capital and a lot of physical effort. Another man digging coal with a gigantic power shovel uses little effort and a great deal of capital. The first would be lucky to produce a few tons in a day; the second might produce more than a hundred. What is measured in the first case is something close to "labor" productivity; there is so little capital involved. The second case deals with "capital" productivity since there is so little labor involved. Yet output in both cases will be expressed in man-hours or man-days, and many will mistakenly refer to both measures as "labor" productivity.

Between 1947 and 1967, the productivity of the U.S. economy more than doubled. This permitted a very large rise in our standard of living. The major cause was technological progress. Other contributing factors were more investment per worker, and the improved quality of the work force due to more and better schooling and improved health services. We invest not only in physical capital, but also in "human capital."

If technology permitted such impressive gains in efficiency in the past, why has productivity faltered in recent years? Edward Renshaw, an economist at the State University of New York at Albany, was one of the first to suggest that technology itself is subject to the law of diminishing returns. His excellent book, *The End of Progress* (Duxbury Press, 1976), has not received the attention from economists it deserves. Renshaw also discussed the causes of declining productivity in a shorter paper published by the Congressional Joint Committee on the Economic Report in a volume called *Economic Growth from 1976–1986: Prospects, Problems, and Patterns* (U.S. Government Printing Office, 1976).

Renshaw was analyzing the problem of declining productivity long before it became a matter of general concern. Technological optimists believe that past trends can be extrapolated indefinitely and that technological progress can go on forever. Renshaw doubts this: "As we near the limits of technological progress," he pointed out in his Joint Committee paper, "it will not be possible to increase one kind of productivity without a sacrifice of some other kind. . . ." That's a new idea, a productivity trade-off.

What are the limits to productivity? Among them Renshaw listed "speed, scale, and the efficiency of converting energy into useful working effects." Traditionally, we have thought of the "efficiency" of transportation in terms of speed. The horseless carriage moved faster than the horse; airplanes moved more swiftly than automobiles. We finally reached the ultimate, excluding space vehicles, in the supersonic transport plane. But is the Concorde efficient? In terms of speed, yes. In terms of fuel consumption per passenger-mile, however, it is incredibly inefficient. The Concorde was developed much too late to make a contribution to technological progress. Even at 1980 fuel prices it was an expensive luxury. Double those prices, and it could become an anachronism. In the future, the efficiency of any mode of transportation will be judged not only in terms of speed but also in terms of energy efficiency.

Renshaw believes that we're approaching—if we have not already reached—the limits of size as a factor contributing to increased productivity. Larger machines, he points out, have been one of the most important sources of increases in productivity. Large factories—and even large organizations—have made similar contributions. But like anything else with an economic dimension, size is subject to the law of diminishing returns. As production is concentrated in fewer and larger units, fuel and raw materials have to be moved longer distances, and products have to be shipped farther to reach their markets. As long as energy prices were constant—or declining relative to other prices—economies of scale probably outweighed incremental transportation costs. But when energy prices began to rise faster than other prices, the cost of transporting materials, energy, and products quickly became a limiting factor on size as a contributor to efficiency.

The number of persons supplied by one farm worker in the U.S. increased from four in 1820 to ten in 1940—a gain of 150 percent. Between 1940 and 1965, a time of rapid mechanization and technological progress in farming, this number jumped from ten to almost fifty—an increase of 400 percent. There will be new technical developments and further increases in farm efficiency, but we will not see another quarter-century like the one starting in 1940. That was a period of increasing returns in farming. Now, because of rising real costs, agriculture is in the more normal state of diminishing returns.

Another example of a major gain in productivity was the 262 percent increase in the coal industry between 1950 and 1969. Later, productivity declined due, primarily, to the twin effects of health and safety regulations and diminishing returns in technology. More recently the trend has been reversed, due to new technical developments in coal mining, but gains in productivity have been relatively small. As in the case of agriculture, we aren't likely to witness another surge in productivity such as that which occurred between 1950 and 1969.

Labor, of course, is a ubiquitous input; it is used in every production process, and we will continue to express productivity in terms of labor time. When interpreting productivity indexes, however, it is important to remember that changes in efficiency are the result of dividing changes in ouput by the entire "bundle" of inputs used in the production process. In most cases, changes in labor time, or labor effort, are the least important of the changes affecting a productivity index.

Productivity and Economic Growth

There's growing agreement that declining productivity is a fundamental cause of national economic stagnation, but why is productivity declining? The nation's leading expert on "growth accounting," Edward F. Denison, has identified several causes. In *Accounting for Slower Economic Growth* (Brookings, 1979), Denison estimated how much of the decline in national income per person employed (NIPPE) could be attributed to changes affecting the basic factors of production—labor, capital, and "land" (where "land" is shorthand for "all natural resources").

The big surprise is that the changes which affected these inputs accounted for only *one-third* of the decline since 1973. The rest is what statisticians call a "residual." Two-thirds of the decline, in other words, can't be "explained" by the variables specifically included in the analysis.

A quick reaction might be that a study which explains only one-third of the change in a highly significant economic indicator can't be given a very high mark, but no one familiar with Denison's distinguished career would denigrate his work. He is one of the trade's outstanding craftsmen. Besides, he doesn't give up easily. The final chapter of this excellent book discusses seventeen potential contributors to the residual, which remains an enigma, if not a mystery, to conventional economists.

Denison's suggestions include: reduced spending on research and development; the decline of "Yankee ingenuity" and the deterioration of American technology; a growing lag in the application of new technical knowledge; aging plant and equipment; government regulations and taxation; lessening competitive pressure; and changes in the quality of management. He also mentions the adverse effects of the rise in energy prices, the shift from the production of goods to services, and "other structural changes" as potential contributors to declining national economic efficiency. This list doesn't exhaust Denison's suggestions, but it includes the more important ones. He doesn't simply list them, but discusses each briefly. Some are rejected. He's skeptical about others. None, he believes, could explain by itself more than a small part of the slowdown. "No single hypothesis," he concludes, "seems to provide a probable explanation of the sharp change after 1973."

In the December 1980 issue of the American Economic Association's *Journal of Economic Literature*, Richard Stone, the leading British authority on national income accounting, comments on Denison's findings. He praises the author's craftsmanship, but wonders if a residual is "really necessary." Stone thinks declining productivity might reflect in part the desire of workers to substitute leisure for income, and he wonders if we don't underestimate true output by failing to count "do-it-yourself" projects in national income. Mainly, however, he believes statisticians should try harder to measure what many now think of as "unmeasurable" economic forces. More and better numbers, he implies, would help whittle down the large residual.

An alternative interpretation of Denison's excellent statistical analysis won't occur to economists who continue to subscribe to the outmoded notions of Neoclassical theory, which continue to dominate the profession. A fundamental tenet of that archaic body of doctrine is that the "normal" state of affairs is steady and continuous economic growth. The decline which Denison has ably documented will be regarded by them as a sign of trouble. The economic machine has jumped off the growth track; something will have to be done to get it back on that track.

The alternative interpretation comes from Nicholas Georgescu-Roegen's bioeconomics. Bioeconomists view the economic system in terms of its biological and physical characteristics rather than as a perpetually growing "machine," and nothing subject to the terrestrial laws of biology and physics can grow without limit. There's no stronger evidence to support Georgescu-Roegen's point of view than Denison's study.

What does this interpretation mean in terms of policy? What should business, government, organized labor—all of us, for that matter—do about this state of affairs? First, we should recognize that it's perfectly natural for mature economies—such as those of Great Britain, the U.S., and other industrialized nations—to slow down. Also, we should realize that we will adapt to the new situation. The economy isn't headed for a breakdown; there is no impending catastrophe. We can live with declining productivity without fear once we realize there's no mystery involved. The "solution" isn't to try to get back to growth rates we will never see again. It is, rather, to discover new ways to divide jobs, the goods and services we produce, and the burden of inflation, equitably.

One of the recurring laments of critics of our political system is the absence of a holistic approach to legislation. Health legislation, environmental legislation, and many other laws, for example, are enacted without regard for possible deleterious productivity consequences. Such legislation is enacted to serve the common good, and it generally does. But it is important to recognize that new laws designed to protect the individual and the environment might have side effects on productivity which will further retard the growth of the national economy.

Health and environmental legislation are not the major causes of declining economic growth. Growing resource and energy scarcities, which lie behind the law of diminishing returns, are far more fundamental causes. But much of the present health and environmental legislation was enacted when rapid economic growth was the order of the day. It is much easier for a robustly growing economy to accommodate such legislation than one in which economic expansion has slowed to a crawl.

Regulation and Productivity

The joint Economic Committee has referred to government regulation as "America's No. 1 growth industry." Expenditures on federal regulatory activities increased from $2.2 billion in 1974 to $4.8 billion in 1978—up 115 percent. Regulation, some critics say, has had a lot to do with declining productivity. Between 1960 and 1973, for example, unit labor costs in manufacturing increased at an average rate of 2.1 percent per year. From 1973 to 1977, however, unit labor cost increases jumped to an average of 7.3 percent per year.

Manufacturing productivity—output per worker-hour—increased by 26.9 percent between 1967 and 1977. That compared with increases of 107 percent in Japan, 72 percent in France, 70 percent in Germany, and 62 percent in Italy. The United Kingdom lagged behind the U.S., with an increase of 26.3 percent, but this difference is negligible. We've heard a lot about the economic woes of Great Britain. In terms of this measure of relative economic performance, however, our record hasn't been much better than theirs.

It's important to qualify the above comparison in two ways. First, wages have gone up faster in other countries than in the U.S., so their unit labor costs also have increased. In Japan, for example, unit labor costs have gone up 215 percent; in France, 106 percent; Germany, 193 percent; Italy, 145 percent; and Great Britain, 99 percent. The increase in the U.S. was only 67 percent. Second, all of the figures given above relate to changes over a recent decade. They tell us nothing about the *absolute level* of productivity in the U.S. compared with other countries.

Denison supports the view that regulation has had adverse effects on productivity. In a study which appeared in *The Survey of Current Business* (January 1978), published by the U.S. Department of Commerce, he stated that pollution abatement rules and health and safety regulations, among others, are "importantly retarding the growth of output per unit of input." Denison's findings are not likely to be disputed. He is a meticulous scholar who documents his conclusions with statistical details. He does not, of course, suggest that regulation is the only, or even the major, cause of the slow rate of economic growth in recent years.

Available evidence—including Denison's *Accounting for Slower Economic Growth*—supports the conclusion that the major cause is the ancient principle of diminishing returns. That principle states that in any production process, output per unit of input goes up rapidly at first, then more slowly. If the relative increase in output is greater than the relative increases in inputs, the result is increasing returns. As an economic system expands, however, the relative increase in output will become smaller than the relative increase in inputs—hence the term "diminishing returns."

Consider a coal mine with a thick seam close to the surface but in which the seam becomes progressively thinner as the mine goes deeper underground. At first this will be a highly productive mine. It could produce fifteen to twenty tons per man-day. Later it will require more time, equipment, and labor to dig each additional ton of coal. Output per man-day might fall to five or six tons. As long as the revenue from each additional ton is greater than its cost, the mine will be operated, but at some point absolutely diminishing returns will set in. There will still be coal in the mine, but it would cost more to produce the remaining coal than it could be sold for, and the mine will be closed.

The same principle applies to all forms of economic activity. As long as there are increasing returns in any production process, there will be rapid growth, but in a finite world nothing grows forever. All growth curves eventually flatten out and look something like an enlongated "S." In economics we generally talk about diminishing returns at the level of the individual company, or even a single plant. But it is becoming increasingly clear that entire economic systems eventually encounter diminishing returns. When this happens, growth rates slow down—sometimes dramatically.

Man-made regulations are subject to modification, but the principle of diminishing returns is immutable. At least, no one has found a way to get around it up to now. If this principle is, in fact, one of the more important causes of the declining rate of economic growth, we are going to have to learn to live with it.

Chapter 7

THE GOVERNMENT'S ROLE
AS WE AND OTHERS SEE IT

European Reactions to Declining Growth

In spite of our sophistication, technological and scientific accomplishments, cultural achievements, and one of the world's higher than average living standards, Americans remain—to use a phrase coined by David Reisman in another context—an "inner-directed" society. We're less curious about other economic systems and their problems than the residents of other countries are about the U.S. It's an interesting exercise, however, to contrast American approaches to the problems discussed in this volume with those found in other democratic societies.

There's been a world of difference, for instance, between the American and Austrian experiences since 1960. The U.S. growth rate—expressed as output per person—averaged 3.4 percent in the 1960s. At that time the Austrian economy grew at 4.5 percent. After 1969, however, the U.S. growth rate dropped to less than 1.5 percent per year, while the Austrian rate increased to 4.7 percent.

Using conventional measures of "living standards"—such as the number of cars, telephones, and television sets per 1,000 people—the United States is still ahead of Austria, but direct comparison of real standards is difficult. The Austrians have access to better public transportation than we, so fewer cars are needed. And the extremes of wealth and poverty, so visible here, aren't found in Austria.

Unlike most other industrialized countries, Austria has managed to avoid "stagflation," to use the lamentable neologism someone has coined to describe rampant inflation coexisting with high-level unemployment. Austria has maintained a stable economy without resorting to comprehensive controls, rationing, or other significant "interferences" in the private sector.

Nominally, the Austrian government is socialist, but Austria doesn't have a centrally-planned economy. Its prosperous and productive farms are privately owned, although farmers use cooperatively owned harvesting and other seasonal equipment. Most businesses are also privately owned and operated. There are a few industrial cities, such as Linz, the steel-making center, but Austria is not as dependent on industry as some of its neighbors. It derives a considerably larger share of its gross product from tourism than do other European countries.

Austria has had a price and incomes policy since the early 1970s, and it works well. That policy, according to the Organization for Economic Cooperation and Development (OECD), is "embedded in a complex system of voluntary and largely informal cooperation between the government and both sides of industry." This means, in brief, that representatives of labor, management, and government set wages and prices simultaneously." It's a system that American labor leaders scorn. They want nothing to do with the "front office." They prefer setting wages by industrial conflict—or the threat of conflict—to cooperation.

To quote the Organization for Economic Cooperation and Development again, Austria's price and income policy "developed in a unique political and historical environment." Austria is a small country. Its population in 1972 was 7.5 million, and the growth rate is only about 21,000 per year. More important, it is culturally homogeneous, and there's a high degree of economic literacy. Austrian political, business, and labor leaders are able to agree on fundamental economic issues because they have the same conception of "the public interest." That doesn't mean orders are issued from above. Austria is a democratic society. Everyone is free to speak, write or criticize at will.

Because of its traditions and homogeneity, the Austrians readily reach consensus on important economic issues. They, along with everyone else in Europe, are appalled that Americans can't come to grips with the energy problem. They know there is an energy problem—for them there always has been one—but they know how to deal with it forthrightly by using energy frugally. Austrians live almost as well as we do, but they consume much less energy per person.

Much has been written about the strength of America's "pluralistic" society. No single economic, ethnic, religious, or other organized group dominates the system. Everyone has a chance to express his or her ideas. Through free discussion we're supposed to reach a consensus, but this becomes harder to do with each new policy issue. That's partly because we now have many well-organized, single-issue groups in the country. Each group wants every other policy issue to revolve around the one it favors. Environmentalists want clean air and water at any cost. Auto owners want cheap gasoline. The anti-nuclear protesters want to end nuclear power generation, and so it goes. The result is anything but harmony. Instead, we have continuous political dissonance.

This will no doubt strike some readers as political heresy of the rankest kind. But the United States can learn something from the nations of Europe which have avoided the problems that are slowly tearing us apart. If we're going to cope at all with the problems engendered by mature industrialism, we'll have to learn to work cooperatively instead of trying to settle all differences by one shoot-out after another at the old corral.

The West German economy is another system which isn't centrally-planned, but remains under control. By contrast, the U.S. economy reminds one of Stephen King's fictional daemonic machines—manglers, lawnmowers, trucks—which become "possessed" and turn on their former human masters. The formerly booming steel industry in the Ruhr basin has slowed down, and this has had negative impacts on the basin's coal producers. For years, during a period of explosive growth, foreign workers were imported from Italy and elsewhere to help man the Ruhr's mines and mills. They're not needed now. There is, in fact, a modest amount of unemployment in the basin. The Germans are realistic about the future of steel, however, since they have watched world capacity grow as developing countries have built their own mills. Now they're searching for alternatives to revitalize the Ruhr economy.

West Germany enjoyed an economic boom for three decades. An entire generation has known nothing but prosperity and rapid economic growth. Now the problem of slow growth looms. With it comes an inevitable concomitant; some regions will enjoy better economic health than others, but the "depressed" parts of Germany look prosperous when compared with depressed areas in other countries. What catches an American eye, when visiting West German cities, is the absence of litter. Streets, sidewalks, public buildings, and transportation systems are well maintained. Shopping areas are bustling. There's an abundance of food and superb beer. There's no visible evidence of poverty. Recent German experience with inflation is one which other industrial countries can regard only with envy. Concern has been expressed that prices have been rising "about 3 percent per year." The United States, by contrast, hasn't had such relative price stability for fifteen years.

What is the problem in West Germany? Essentially, it's that the Ruhr unemployment rate is now approaching the U.S. average of the past few years. But where our lawmakers have come to regard 6 percent or higher unemployment with equanimity, political leaders in the Ruhr are concerned when it gets much above 3 percent. As in Austria, there is a high degree of cooperation, and a great deal of free discussion among the representatives of various economic groups. Because of this, Germany could be one of the first industrial nations to adapt to slow growth without either excessive unemployment or inflation.

One often wonders why public officials or aspirants to high public office in the United States seem unable to speak with the candor of their British or Western European counterparts. Are we more innocent or more gullible than the British or the French? It's natural for a challenger to stress the ineptness of an incumbent, but does criticism of the opposition preclude realistic statements about the economy? It doesn't in other countries. It seems to here.

An interview with then President Valery Giscard d'Estaing of France, reported in *Paris Match* (September 14, 1979), attracted considerable attention in this country. It's easy to see why. It makes refreshing reading compared with the banal pronouncements of most American politicians.

The subject was the role of France in a world that has undergone a major transformation during the past decade or so. American politicians outdo one another in promising a return to the days of rapid economic growth and rising expectations. Giscard, by contrast, said: "The truth is that we cannot return to the way it was before. What we must do is to try to adapt to another situation." To provide leadership in a world of slow growth and declining economic expectations, Giscard has suggested a maxim which all governments could wisely follow: "The government must clearly define this policy of facing reality, and do so in plain language. It must avoid two pitfalls: illusion, which eliminates effort, and pessimism, which discourages undertaking."

Giscard believes that the "consumer society"—which many thought would last indefinitely—has come to an end. He thinks it lasted in France from 1960 to 1973. It started earlier here, and few will admit that it has ended, but the harsh reality of inflation is beginning to cut into the American standard of living. Sooner or later, as the French already have done, we'll have to lower our expectations. French attitudes toward slow growth, and their efforts to cope with it, reflect a realistic approach to the economic process. During the early 1960s the French pioneered an approach to management of the economy called "indicative" or "non-coercive" planning.

The complete process is complex and won't be described here, but it's really the underlying philosophy that's important. The objective was to bring together, periodically, leaders of all organized groups to establish tentative production targets for major economic sectors. Economists and other technicians provided the projections. Industry representatives estimated the amounts they would have to produce to reach the projected targets. Representatives of management, unions, and government discussed wages, prices and productivity to set the stage for later collective bargaining.

Because it was open and democratic, indicative planning was observed with interest on this side of the Atlantic. The Committee for Economic Development—a private association of U.S. business interests—distributed a report on the role of private enterprise in the preparation of the plan. Indicative planning didn't work as well as its supporters had hoped it would, partly because present economic forecasting methods leave much to be desired. Technicians weren't able to make reliable estimates of the foreign demand for French products. They also couldn't work out all of the regional and other internal ramifications of changes in major sectors. But the French haven't given up. A group of French economists is working on a model of the economy which will tie all regions into a single unified system. It's what we call a "bottom-up" interregional model in this country. Information is gathered at the regional level. Later, the regional numbers are added to obtain national totals. Once completed, the model should contribute to more successful indicative planning.

Attitudes are more important than the technical aspects of indicative planning. Giscard maintained that the French were never completely happy with the "consumer society." That is why they don't lament its passing. In this country, by contrast, each politician tries to pipe a more cheerful tune. Only after elections do we—like the children of Hamelin—discover illusion, as promises give way to the realities of modern economic life.

Some political scientists lament the piecemeal approach to public policy which is a hallmark of the American system. Unlike French indicative planning, where the *interdependence* of all sectors of the economy is recognized, the U.S. approach has been to attack economic problems seriatim. The result is a set of policies that often are at cross purposes. It would require a volume many times the size of this one to discuss this problem comprehensively. The following sections serve only to illustrate the point.

Federal Employment Policy

Federal involvement in training programs started on a small scale in 1961 when John F. Kennedy signed his first major law, the Area Redevelopment Act. That law authorized, among other things, annual appropriations of $4.5 million for vocational training, and $10 million for subsistence payments. In 1974 the combined budgets of federal jobs programs, by then transferred to a special branch of the Department of Labor, the Manpower Administration, were $5 billion. In 1980 they added up to more than $15 billion.

The centerpiece of the jobs program was established in 1973 by the Comprehensive Employment and Training Act (CETA). It accounted for 60 percent of manpower spending in 1980. CETA had many critics and few defenders. Its most vocal critics were those whose minds had been numbed by Proposition 13 fever. The symptom identifying this malady is the unshakeable belief that taxes are an unmitigated evil. Knee-jerk critics of CETA didn't want to reform it; they wanted to abolish it. Let the "welfare loafers" supported by productive, tax-paying private citizens, they said, learn skills and find jobs on their own. Such criticism might relieve pressure on the spleen. It has little effect on politicians.

The proliferation of federal manpower programs raised policy issues, however, which call for serious discussion. When Congress expanded training and related programs in 1974, the Manpower Administration's staff couldn't manage all the new activities. Since the civil service system moves slowly and Congress wants fast results—so candidates can bring them to the attention of voters during election campaigns—CETA administrators turned to the private sector for help. They got the expanded programs off the ground by supporting "nonprofit intermediaries" to manage some of their demonstration, youth incentive, and other activities. This, in effect, created a hidden bureaucracy.

Nonprofit intermediaries can be staffed quickly, and they're free of the red tape that hamstrings official government activities. But the use of outside consulting firms has been questioned by critics, including some who are not hostile toward federal job programs. There are palpable risks involved—favoritism, cost overruns, the danger of corruption, to name a few. Once established, the intermediaries keep funding pipelines to government agencies open. They aren't bound by job freezes, so hiring is limited only by the size of federal grants. They become an unofficial arm of government—

subject to considerably less supervision than official agencies.

Nonprofit intermediaries have been defended by Eli Ginsburg, a leading expert on manpower problems. Congress, he says, "is often schizophrenic: It makes more programs and more funds available to an agency, but it puts serious obstacles in the way of their obtaining additional staff." By limiting the official bureaucracy it literally forces agencies to expand the hidden bureaucracy.

Most congressmen prefer to see funds "pass through" federal agencies to state and local governments. But the agencies prefer nonprofit intermediaries, especially when research and development are involved. They have some control over the nonprofit organizations funded, but little or none over state and local governments.

An inevitable consequence of overfunding and understaffing is a proliferation of consulting firms. Many of these are legitimate. They do good research and perform work that bureaucrats frequently aren't qualified to do. Others are "feather merchants" who specialize in useless fluff delivered in attractive bindings. The real dilemma is that many bureaucrats and congressmen aren't capable of distinguishing between the two.

Regional Development Policy

Did the country need a new layer of government—one between Washington and the state capitols? Supporters of "wall-to-wall" regional commissions evidently believe that it did. They came close to translating that belief into reality.

Two kinds of regional development commissions were established in the United States by the Kennedy and Johnson administrations, in addition to several sets of regions established earlier for purely statistical purposes. One is the unique Appalachian Regional Commission. The domain of the ARC includes all of West Virginia and parts of twelve other states. It was established in 1965, initially to tie Appalachia to the rest of the nation via a system of development highways linked to the interstate system. Three-fourths of the proposed 2,233 miles of development highways have been completed or are under construction. Engineering and right-of-way work is in progress on the remainder.

Once the development highways were assured, the ARC shifted its emphasis to "investment in human capital." This is the crass term economists use to describe investments designed to improve the efficiency of human beings. Practically, it means an effort to improve education and the delivery of health services.

The ARC invested substantial amounts in vocational education and health facilities, and in demonstration health programs, including those concerned with child development. Smaller amounts were spent on reclamation projects and housing. Federal grants required some matching state funds, so the total investment in ARC projects was larger than the federal contribution.

During its early days ARC was roundly criticized by some economists; the development highway program, in particular, was characterized as a gigantic boondoggle. There is wide agreement now that the ARC made a difference in the region. It has been helped tremendously, of course, by the revival of coal, but ARC is now given high marks even by some former critics.

The other regional commissions are not as well known as the ARC. They are the Regional Action Planning Commissions, authorized by the Public Works and Economic Development Act of 1965. In bureaucratic circles they are called "Title V Commissions," after the section of the law which permitted them to come into existence.

The 1965 Act didn't designate specific commissions; it enabled groups of contiguous states which desired to do so to establish them. Within a year five had been set up. They were: the Ozarks, New England, Four Corners, Coastal Plains, and Upper Great Lakes. Like the ARC, Title V Commissions have federal co-chairmen. Unlike ARC, their headquarters aren't in Washington.

Not much is known about the activities of the Title V commissions. Some critics say they deliberately maintain low profiles. Through the years the New England Commission came to be known as the "best" of the Title V's. In October 1972, however, the *Boston Globe* published a series of four articles about the New England Commission.

The first article was headlined, "Do-Nothing Bureaucracy Squanders Millions of Tax Dollars." Those articles—which are outstanding examples of investigative journalism—make discouraging reading for anyone committed to the notion of federally sponsored regional development programs. The *Globe*, incidentally, is Boston's liberal newspaper. In this set of articles it was attacking by indirection the politicians it generally supports.

One of the more interesting revelations of the *Globe* articles is that the New England governors had subverted the legislative intent of the 1965 Act. Like the ARC, Title V commissions were supposed to promote regionwide projects. In practice, the governors used the New England Commission to funnel federal funds directly to their states. There was no scandal, no question about the legitimacy of this form of "revenue sharing." But there was little or no regionwide coordination—nothing comparable to the Appalachian Development Highway System. The other original Title V commissions haven't received the kind of attention given the New England Commission, for which their respective co-chairmen must be everlastingly grateful. They also haven't received any favorable comment in the journals that typically discuss regional affairs. Their accomplishments, if any, have attracted no attention.

One of the Carter administration's less notable accomplishments—which also received practically no publicity—was to expand the number of Title V commissions. For practical purposes, the nation was given a set of "wall-to-wall" regional planning commissions. Like the original set of commissions, they haven't distinguished themselves by engaging in either regional "planning" or regional development.

How did the new, nearly invisible, layer of government get slipped by the public so easily? Largely because it had the support of the nation's governors. It became one more way of channeling federal funds to the states. Almost anything a governor wants to do can be described as "economic development," since this is a highly elastic notion, and the federal funds come with virtually no strings attached.

A strong case can be made for federal involvement in regional economic affairs. But such involvement did not require a new layer of bureaucrats who did little more than shuffle funds and paper between Washington and the states. If revenue sharing is what Congress and the states wanted, why didn't they do it openly and as efficiently as possible? The experience of Title V commissions strongly suggests that this approach to revenue sharing certainly isn't in the "public interest"—however that elusive term is defined.

Pollution and Its Abatement

Every state has at least one agency promoting economic growth. This is done by encouraging—and sometimes subsidizing—the location of new manufacturing or other processing activities in the state. The benefits of industrial growth are taken for granted by development agencies. They include new jobs, higher incomes, more taxes, and often more public conveniences.

Until the late 1960s these benefits were seldom if ever questioned. In *Goals for Americans*, a 1960 report to President Eisenhower prepared by a star-studded citizens' commission, growth, industrialization, and technological progress were cited as the hope of the future. Nowhere was there mention of pollution or the environment. Less than ten years later there were federal laws designed to reduce the amounts of chemicals and detritus in the air, as well as scum, sewage, and debris in the nation's inland waters.

Was there no pollution before the late 1960s? Of course there was. Industrial cities, such as Pittsburgh, were heavily polluted. And there were sporadic outcries against the "social costs" created by industrialists during the accumulation of private profits. But it wasn't until the 1962 publication of Rachel Carson's *Silent Spring*—a book noted for its literary grace as well as its startling revelations about the environmental effects of pesticides—that an ecological "movement" was born.

Even without Carson's elegiac book, concern about the environment would have been one of the ineluctable consequences of the 1960s—the most unusual decade in the nation's economic history. Never before had the United States experienced such sustained and robust economic growth. Since pollution was a byproduct of rapid growth—and the rampant consumerism it engendered—one might have imagined that economists would have prescribed slower growth, but they didn't. The standard prescription was for faster growth which would permit new technological solutions to environmental problems.

Conventional economists said the problem could be handled by "internalizing the externalities" of pollution. This jargon means that industrialists could install pollution abatement devices—inventing new ones when necessary. The cost would be paid out of the nation's "growth dividend." We could, they assured us, have the best of both worlds—rapid economic growth as well as clean air and water.

The basic assumption was that the growth of the 1960s would continue, but it hasn't. There was little growth during the 1970s. Without growth there can be no "growth dividend," and the facile recommendation that industrialists bear the full cost of pollution abatement isn't heard these days—at least not from reputable economists. They talk about "trade-offs." If the nation is to enjoy the benefits of industrialization, it will have to bear some of the costs.

The ancient trade-off formula answers some questions, but it raises new ones. Who will enjoy the benefits? Who pays the costs? If the benefits are national or regional, should a single community pay in terms of environmental degradation? How much pollution will be added by new processes still on drawing boards—especially those designed to augment energy supplies?

A recent study, "Coal Conversion Technologies: Some Health and Environmental Effects," sheds light on the latter critical question. It was conducted at the Brookhaven Laboratory and published in *Science* (November 9, 1979). The report is too long and technical to be reviewed in detail here. Its authors explicitly recognized the potential environmental hazards of four coal conversion processes not yet in use, however, and compared them with four combustion systems currently available.

All of their emissions estimates were derived from a computerized "simulation" model developed earlier at the Brookhaven Laboratory. They aren't necessarily the last word on the subject. But the model is a sophisticated one which includes the entire fuel cycle from extraction to final use. As coal conversion plants are completed, observed emissions can be compared with those projected by the model. Such studies show that we aren't going into coal conversion "in the blind." If hazards are recognized and dealt with in advance, they can be minimized. Almost any industrial process will have some deleterious environmental effects. But it's important to distinguish between "nuisance effects" and those that are really harmful.

Like the Luddites, who tried to stem the Industrial Revolution by attacking machines, some objectors to the expansion of industrial activities considered to be potential polluters have vented their anger by harassing construction crews or vandalizing equipment. Everyone appears to agree that industrialization is a Good Thing. But a corollary of this attitude seems to be that the plants should always be located somewhere else.

Science and Public Policy

Are some federal policies based on incomplete or untested scientific findings? There has been some concern in the scientific community that this is so, particularly in the health and environmental areas. Two articles which appeared in *Science* deal with this issue.

Most scientists are conservative about publishing research findings. Research results are subjected to peer review before appearing in scholarly and technical journals. Even published results are not always accepted as the last word. Scientific journals contain examples of lively debate on controversial scientific issues.

Since the late 1960s a number of federal laws have been enacted dealing with health and environmental matters. Those laws produced a web of new regulations, and created new bureaucracies to administer them. The laws were designed to protect the commonweal. No one doubts the sincerity or integrity of their sponsors and supporters. Health and environmental regulations are not determined arbitrarily or capriciously by congressional staff members; they are based on studies conducted by government agencies. But is it possible that some of the findings upon which new laws are based are premature or incomplete? Whether it's happening or not, the possibility can't be denied.

Cyril Comar, a retired Cornell University professor, stated that "bad science, especially in the environmental and health areas, may well impose socioeconomic penalties hardly envisioned" (*Science*, June 16, 1978). Later, M. Granger Morgan, head of the Department of Engineering and Public Policy at Carnegie-Mellon University, stated that "bad science . . . is leading to unwarranted public concerns, unjustified and costly regulatory action, and serious public misunderstanding" (*Science*, September 15, 1978).

The term "bad science" refers to scientific results that have not been adequately tested or reviewed. The goal of "good science" is the discovery of objective truth. Personal preferences and personal values have nothing to do with objective truth, but often have a great deal to do with the determination of public policy.

When lawmakers deal with health and environmental matters, they are dealing with issues that arouse strong emotions—perhaps more than in any area of policy concern, excluding war. Powerful lobbies have been formed to press for legislation against many things that are hazardous to our health. No one in his right mind would argue in favor of health hazards. But do lawmakers always know what is hazardous? Some scientists feel they don't and that they are legislating on the basis of incomplete and imperfect data.

There would be no problem if health and environmental legislation had no undesirable side-effects. But it is clear that such legislation has had effects on the economy which were not intended, and some of which were not foreseen. The sulfur standard in the Clean Air Act of 1975 is one example among many that could be chosen.

No one knows for certain that burning coal which contains 3.5 percent sulfur is injurious to health, or just how injurious it might be. That level was not determined after exhaustive scientific study under conditions that would remove all doubt about the injurious nature of high-sulfur coal. But fully documented and tested information was not available when the law was written, and still is not. The 3.5 percent sulfur level was adopted as a "reasonable" standard. It might be too high, or it might be too low. Although scientists are not certain about this, one can find support for either position. Careful studies could and should be conducted to determine the effects of higher and lower standards.

Professor Morgan feels that the answer to the problem of bad science is to improve the capability of policy analysts. Policy analysis examines the complete implications of alternative courses of action. A sound policy analysis of environmental legislation would definitely look at health and health-related issues. It would also examine the direct and indirect costs of various proposals. An effort would be made to set standards and devise regulations which would maximize benefits while minimizing costs.

Part of the problem is that people skilled in policy analysis are not necessarily skilled in science and engineering. Professor Morgan believes there is a need to train some scientists and engineers in policy analysis. This, of course, is a long-run approach to the problem. In the meantime there is no reason why government studies, which are to be used as the basis for legislation, should not be subject to the same peer review that determines whether or not private studies find their way into print. Laws based on scientific studies would actually be strengthened if their standards and regulations had been approved by an impartial scientific jury.

One expects criticism of health and environmental laws from those whose vested interests are harmed. The tobacco industry, for example, will never be cheerful about government efforts to curb smoking. But when impartial scientists express concern about bad science and public policy, the rest of us should listen.

Coordinating Federal Policies— The Case for Indicative Planning

The preceding sections are little more than policy vignettes. The policies briefly described deal with issues that are interrelated, but the policies themselves are not. There are connections between employment, unemployment, regional development, control of the environment, and one could go on to list dozens of other issues which engage the attention of government officials. As noted earlier, however, legislation on one issue is enacted and administered with virtually complete disregard for all other issues.

A completely justified complaint about government is that individual federal programs do not add up to a common goal— however desirable the specific objectives of each program. In some cases the objectives of two policies are in direct opposition. This is so, for example, when the goals of health, safety, and environmental laws are contrasted with efforts to stimulate productivity. Each objective is desirable. So are the advantages of full employment, educational opportunities for the disadvantaged, decent housing for all, less crime, an adequate—but not excessive—defense establishment, and so on. But every one of these desirable goals comes into partial conflict with some other desirable objective. So how do policy-makers choose among them?

In today's complex, pluralistic society there are many special-interest and single-issue groups. Some are highly organized, well-financed, and extremely vocal lobbies. They bombard Congress with information and propaganda. In an earlier day when life was simpler, lobbies were regarded as the bane of democracy. That was when most lobbies represented business interests. But "public-interest" groups have made the institution of lobbying respectable. Some political scientists now regard lobbies as an essential part of the democratic process.

Individual lawmakers have to pick and choose among pressure groups since they represent conflicting interests. Senators and congressmen support the parochial interests of their states. On broader issues, such as foreign aid, defense expenditures, and similar global matters, they are more susceptible to the blandishments of special-interest organizations.

What's missing in our system of government is a central clearinghouse for the evaluation of alternative proposals. Some corporations are now experimenting with "matrix management." This is an attempt to see how the functions of different departments are interrelated. Engineers, for example, don't focus exclusively on the technical aspects of their work. They deal with budget considerations at the same time they are working on design problems. Accountants, meanwhile, try to anticipate the effects of current research expenditures on future earnings. This is one form of "systems analysis" in which an effort is made to look at all the components of the system simultaneously. Federal programs could be coordinated in a similar manner.

Coordination won't be enough, however, if the American political and economic systems are to survive in anything resembling their present forms. If that is to happen, the trend started by the Reagan administration to reduce government involvement in the economy will have to be reversed. Instead of trying to get as close as possible to *laissez faire*, the federal government will have to be an active participant in a program of democratic, or "indicative," planning. That would require establishment of a national planning commission which would include representatives of government, labor, management, agriculture, education, and any other group whose actions could have an impact on the economy.

Several years ago Congress established an Office of Technology Assessment (OTA) to help members understand technical and scientific issues on which they have to legislate. It hasn't been an unqualified success, but the OTA has helped lawmakers deal with matters they couldn't understand without technical guidance. There would be no need for a new agency, however, to coordinate and evaluate the economic impacts of proposed federal programs or of the elimination of existing programs. That could be done jointly by the Council of Economic Advisers, on the executive side, and the Congressional Budget Office, on the legislative side. Together, these agencies could make up an Office of Impact Evaluation (OIE). The OIE could also serve as the government's representative on a national planning commission.

What is "indicative" planning? What distinguishes it from economic planning as it is practiced, for example, in the Soviet Union? The most important difference is that it is *noncoercive*. It is a completely democratic and voluntary process. In the United States the word "planning" has a negative connotation. It's hard to imagine, however, a private business—or any private organization—functioning successfully without some form of planning. But the word is anathema to politicians, especially at the federal level.

One of the more articulate advocates of indicative planning is Wassily Leontief, who won the Nobel Prize in Economic Science in 1973 for the development of input-output analysis. The basis of Leontief's analytical method is a large transactions table—a statistical grid whose rows show sales by every sector of the economy to every other sector. The columns of the grid simultaneously show purchases by every sector from every other sector. The table shows, in brief, how every sector depends upon every other sector; it shows the *interdependence* of all units that make up an economic system.

The input-output system, unlike conventional economic "models," is compatible with any kind of political system. Every major country, and many smaller nations, now construct input-output tables on a regular basis. Some do a better job than others. It is ironic that the U.S.—the birthplace of input-output analysis—now lags behind a number of other countries in the timeliness and size of its input-output tables. As Leontief pointed out to the Congressional Joint Economic Committee on January 19, 1982, countries whose economic performance has far outstripped that of the United States during the past decade have more comprehensive and better coordinated statistical systems than we do. They also—and this is no coincidence— engage in indicative planning. Examples include Japan, Austria, and Norway.

There is no fixed formula for indicative planning, and there is only one requirement; it must be carried out in a democratic fashion. Indicative planning does not eliminate markets; it makes them function more effectively. The following discussion of how indicative planning might work in the United States is a composite based on the experience of several countries. It draws to some extent on Leontief's statement to the Joint Economic Committee. It is, of course, only a summary of the process.

The national planning commission, as indicated earlier, would be made up of representatives of all groups who can influence the economy by their actions. There would be a small technical staff of economists and statisticians. Their role would be to provide the commission with timely, accurate economic *information*. They would play no role in the decision-making process.

The first step would be to evaluate the recent performance of the economy, and to make a series of economic projections based on a set of alternative scenarios. The assumptions behind each projection would be clearly stated by the economists and statisticians involved. The projections would, of course, link the United States economy to the rest of the world. They would be used by members of the commission in discussions, debate, and negotiations conducted to arrive at a consensus on what and how much was to be produced, and how the output of the economy was to be distributed. The words to stress in the last sentence are *negotiations* and *consensus*.

Why would the commission need another forecast? We already have a surfeit. Toward the end of each year *Business Week* summarizes a score of forecasts made by individual business economists, as well as several projections made by a number of consulting organizations using econometric models. Typically, they range from a few excessively optimistic forecasts—which could be realized only by a revival of the robust growth of the 1960s—to one that might border on pessimism. A forecast can be found to support almost any point of view. That's why forecasting as it's now practiced does little more than perpetuate the canard that if you laid all the economists in the country end to end they wouldn't reach a conclusion.

How would this change under indicative planning? Would forecasts by individual economists or consulting firms be prohibited? Not at all. The technical staff of the national planning commission might want to examine the entire array of published forecasts and to learn as much as it could about the assumptions on which they are based. Most forecasters work with the same data. Their results differ because they make different assumptions.

Under indicative planning an effort would be made to reach a consensus on assumptions by participants in the planning process before detailed forecasts were made by the technical staff. Each representative on the planning commission would have his or her say. Differences would be ironed out by discussion, not by edict. What if the participants couldn't agree? No problem. The technical staff could make several forecasts, and the reasonableness of different assumptions could be evaluated after the fact.

At some point a consensus would have to be reached, just as settlements are finally agreed upon where there is successful collective bargaining. True, more than two parties would be involved in the planning process. But a consensus would result from negotiation, persuasion, and above all constant reference to known facts. Indicative planning would work, of course, only where there was a willingness to reach agreement. And one cannot stress too much that any agreement, once reached, would not be binding on any of the constituencies represented on the planning commission. Indicative planning is a cooperative affair, not a coercive one.

Members of the planning commission would not have to agree on all the details of the forecast. They would first have to agree on projected "sales to final demand," or a detailed "bill of goods" representing estimates by industry experts of how much each sector would sell to households, government, and foreign buyers in the target year. They would also have to agree on the volume of production needed for capital formation; that is, the amounts sold by each sector to others which produce capital goods—buildings, machinery, equipment, and so on—to be used for production rather than current consumption.

Once the commission agreed on a set of projections of final demand, the technical staff would take over. The earlier projections would be fed into an input-output model which consists of sets of coefficients. Leontief has described the latter as "cooking recipes." Technical coefficients indicate how much of each input is needed to produce a unit of output; for example, how much iron ore, coal, limestone, electric power, and all other inputs are needed to produce one ton of steel. Labor coefficients would indicate how much labor would be required. Finally, capital coefficients would show how much each sector would have to invest in plant expansion, if the final demand forecasts indicate the need for new capacity, as well as the amounts needed to replace worn-out plant and equipment.

The forecasts summarized in *Business Week* each year deal only in broad aggregates and averages. Even when they hit the mark—which few do—they provide only limited information. The hallmark of input-output projections, by contrast, is that they're highly detailed. They show not only the total projected output of each industry or other sector of the economy, but the direct and indirect requirements for producing that output.

The input-output model could be used to conduct "experiments" by computer simulation. By altering the assumption upon which projections are based, it is possible to evaluate the impacts of alternative government policies. A wide range of alternatives could be explored and evaluated.

It's easy to observe the direct effects of a change in a specific government policy. If expenditures for Aid to Dependent Children are reduced by a certain amount, for instance, it's a simple matter to calculate the initial income losses in each state. An input-output model would provide additional information, however, since it would trace the *indirect* effects of this specific cut in government spending on income and employment. Similarly, the indirect effects of a decline in production in the private sector—in the automobile industry, for example—would be estimated by the model. It requires little imagination to see how such economic "experiments" would be less painful than many of those actually carried out by government when it makes fundamental changes in existing policies.

The Reagan administration undertook, for example, to reverse the fiscal policies of the Carter and earlier administrations. One consequence of cutbacks in federal spending was a substantial increase in unemployment. A rise in unemployment means, of course, that consumer spending will fall. This contributes further to unemployment in the private sector. It was not President Reagan's intention to add to the nation's economic woes. He had been led to believe by his "supply-side" advisers that tax and spending cuts would stimulate, not further depress, the economy. How much less painful it would have been for all concerned if the impacts of the tax and spending cuts had been simulated by a computer rather than being experienced by the victims of an unsound economic theory.

Would indicative planning turn the economy around? Would it achieve the goal of robust growth which has eluded every administration since the euphoric Kennedy years? There is no reason to think it would. Planning cannot affect the second law of thermodynamics, nor would it repeal the economic law of diminishing returns. The conventional view is that unemployment, inflation, declining productivity, and so on are purely *economic* problems, and thus can be "solved" when the correct *economic* policies are put into effect.

The Reagan administration claims that the economic problems of the early 1980s were caused by the mistaken policies of its predecessors. Critics claim that Reaganomics has exacerbated problems which their policies would have corrected. No one in a position of authority is willing to admit that these problems might be beyond the control of any policy based on conventional economic principles.

Then why plan? If the outlook is hopeless, what difference does it make? Responsible critics of conventional economics have not suggested that the outlook is hopeless. They have argued instead that conventional economics—no matter how well it might have performed in the past—has outlived its usefulness. It's time to adopt a new and, by present definition, unconventional approach.

If the revival of robust economic growth were physically possible, if the world were not faced with a severe and worsening problem of energy and resource constraints, the case for indicative planning might be weaker. But declining economic growth—with all the problems it has engendered—is not a uniquely American experience. It is a worldwide phenomenon, and the world is now well into the second decade of this new and disturbing condition.

If indicative planning can't revive economic growth, what can it do? Perhaps one of the more important contributions democratic planning could make—because of its emphasis on observed facts, rather than competing abstract theories—would be to introduce a note of realism now sadly lacking in the pronouncements of American political leaders. If the members of a national planning commission were convinced that growth is not the cure-all it is supposed to be, it could turn its attention to other national goals. One of the more important of the latter would be to insure employment opportunities for everyone able and willing to work.

Neither unemployment nor uncontrollable inflation need be tolerated by a society willing to substitute cooperation for Adam Smith's "invisible hand." Unlike energy and natural resources, the world will not run out of useful work. By a democratic, cooperative effort, available work could be shared by those willing to perform it. That would require a more equitable distribution of what we produce than we've had in the past. But this too will come if our society is to survive.

There are a few faint glimmerings that we might be approaching a new era of cooperation. A. H. Raskin, a veteran labor reporter, recently wrote about "The Cooperative Economy," (*New York Times*, February 14, 1982). "Confrontation," he said, "has gone out of fashion. In a troubled economy, unions and companies are finding that each must give a little." Raskin shows that in several basic industries—including rubber, steel, airlines, and trucking—unions are willing to forego wage increases to protect jobs. This is a new turn of events. It might well foreshadow a cooperative approach to a broader range of economic problems. Increasing cooperation between former antagonists suggests a willingness to recognize that the economy is not a huge gambling table. It's a system in which the fortunes of each member of society depend in an intricate and generally very indirect way on those of every other member. The name of that game is not economic roulette; it's indicative planning.

This chapter has introduced a policy proposal which is conjoined with Georgescu-Roegen's bioeconomics. It is Leontief's version of indicative planning, which would make extensive use of the input-output system he invented. This analytical tool is now used in Japan, Austria, and Norway, where indicative planning is practiced with a high degree of success. More will be said about this merger of ideas in the final chapter.

Chapter 8

CHOICES FOR THE FUTURE

The Evolution of Scientific Thought

A common view of science is that it consists of a series of finished modules piled on top of one another. We know that scientific development is an evolutionary process, and most of us learn about the great discoveries of science in elementary school, particularly those which have had economic or medical applications, such as the steam engine or polio vaccine. It's likely that laymen who trouble themselves about the matter at all view the evolution of scientific *thought* in the same manner, but the situation isn't that simple. The development of scientific thought is anything but a smooth process or steady progression of ideas neatly stacked on one another.

Lewis Thomas, who heads the Memorial Sloan-Kettering Cancer Center in New York, has done as much as anyone to dispel some of the myths about the nature of science. Two collections of his essays, which first appeared in the *New England Journal of Medicine*, were published as books which became best sellers: *The Lives of a Cell* (The Viking Press, 1974) and *The Medusa and the Snail* (The Viking Press, 1979). His most penetrating thoughts about the evolution of science appeared in a short article, however, in the September–October 1980 issue of *Harvard Magazine*.

"The great body of science," Thomas said, "built like a vast hill over the past 300 years, is a mobile, unsteady structure." The entire arrangement of scientific thought, he went on, exhibits "something like the unpredictability and unreliability of living flesh." There's a lot of trial and error in scientific thinking. Science is not, as is sometimes thought, "a way of building a solid indestructable body of immutable truths . . . it keeps changing, shifting, revising, discovering that it was wrong and then heaving itself explosively apart to redesign everything. It is a living thing, a celebration of human fallibility."

Thomas was talking, of course, about the evolution of what are commonly called the hard sciences: physics, chemistry, biology, and so forth. But what he said applies even more to the social sciences. Unfortunately, that's not the way the social sciences are usually taught, which is one reason we make so little progress in adapting to a constantly changing world. "We are in trouble," Thomas says, "whenever persuaded that we know everything." The general public, however, including many college graduates, is likely to have an exaggerated notion of how far we've progressed in our understanding of the complex world in which we live. "The culmination of a liberal arts education," Thomas says, "ought to include the news that we do not understand a flea much less the making of a thought."

Economists are as guilty as any scholarly group of creating the impression that theirs is a highly developed discipline, that it comes close to being a finished product. As in the physical sciences, however, there have been vast changes in economic doctrine. The changes do not come easily. In 1935 John Maynard Keynes wrote: "The difficulty lies, not in the new ideas, but in escaping from the old ones, which ramify, for those brought up as most of us have been, into every corner of our minds." Those are without doubt the most prescient words written by the great British economist.

The "Keynesian Revolution," as it is still called, was his demonstration that, contrary to received doctrine prior to his time, free enterprise economies are not self-equilibrating systems. Keynes argued that as an economy matures it can settle down in a "false" equilibrium; there can be chronic high-level unemployment for an indefinite period. An unregulated economy will not eliminate such unemployment. Keynes concluded that the government could close the gap by maintaining investment and consumer spending at full-employment levels. The idea of such government involvement in the economy was shocking in 1935. It is accepted orthodoxy today.

Keynes didn't trouble himself about such mundane matters as the supply of energy and resources. He concerned himself entirely with demand problems, and he taught us how to solve those problems. As Georgescu-Roegen has pointed out, however, today's problems are supply problems. We would know how to maintain effective demand at full-employment levels—without inflation—in a world which had a completely inexhaustible supply of energy and resources. That, in essence, is the kind of world Keynes assumed we lived in. But we know now that's not true.

A fundamental conclusion of bioeconomics is that mankind will be forced to adjust to a steady diminution in the availability of energy and nonrenewable resources. This is a far more revolutionary notion than Keynes's conclusion that mature free market economies were not self-equilibrating. It is being resisted even more strongly than Keynes's teachings in the late 1930s. Even if one is convinced on intellectual grounds that economic growth can't go on indefinitely, the idea is definitely lacking in emotional appeal. Because it is the only analysis of the economic process which is built on a solid foundation of biological and thermodynamic reality, however, it will become the economic orthodoxy of the future.

Bioeconomics has made more headway in Western Europe than in the United States. Two of Georgescu-Roegen's papers, which together provide a concise summary of his basic ideas, appeared in France in 1979 as a book entitled *Demain la Décroissiance* (Paris: Pierre-Marcel, Favre), with a preface and introduction by Ivo Rens and Jacques Grinevald. A considerably longer book, *Georgescu-Roegen*, was published by Stefano Zamagni in Italy (Milan: Estas Libri, 1979). It includes a comprehensive bibliography of Georgescu-Roegen's writings through 1978.

American resistance to the revolutionary ideas of bioeconomics might be due to a combination of hedonistic and intellectual influences. Rampant consumerism has never been as deeply ingrained in the cultures of Great Britain and Western Europe as it has been in the United States. The idea that thrift is a virtue—a notion which Keynes did his best to dispel—is more deeply imbedded in European culture than it ever has been in the United States. Thus the notion that economic growth might not go on forever may be less traumatic for many Europeans than for most Americans.

It would be worse than misleading—it would be completely wrong—to suggest that Georgescu-Roegen's ideas have had no impact on the intellectual community in the United States. They have been the subject of feature articles in *Science* and in the American Chemical Society's *Chemical and Engineering News*. His book, *The Entropy Law and the Economic Process*, is widely regarded as a modern classic. Half of the contributors to a *Festschrift* published in his honor are Nobel laureates in economics.

Two of Georgescu-Roegen's major articles were published in the *Southern Economic Journal*, a publication which ranks as one of the leading journals in its field. But one can still conclude that while the "Economics Establishment" has been quick to honor the man and his powerful and stimulating intellect, it has staunchly resisted acceptance of the principles of bioeconomics. Those principles have not been attacked in the major journals of the economics profession; they have simply been ignored.

The reason isn't hard to find. Earlier ideas which shook the foundations of traditional economics—and which met initial resistance—turned out, on more careful examination, to be less revolutionary than was originally thought. They could be incorporated into the ever-expanding corpus of accepted economic doctrine. It's true that each of the new theories—or paradigms—had to overcome resistance. Their acceptance was gradual rather than sudden and probably never was complete. Examples are Edward Chamberlain's theory of monopolistic competition and Keynes's general theory of employment, interest, and money. Those ideas have been assimilated by today's conventional economics through the process described by Lewis Thomas in his discussion of the evolution of science. Some old ideas had to be discarded, and others had to be modified. Once this process was completed, however, a later generation of economists would have expressed surprise that what had become orthodox in economics had ever been in dispute.

Will the principles of bioeconomics gradually work their way into the "mainstream" of conventional economic thought as other new departures have in the past? Unfortunately, they won't. The fundamental irreconcilability between the basic principles of bioeconomics and several of the central tenets of conventional economics was pointed out in Chapter 1. One cannot view the economic process in mechanistic and biological-thermodynamic terms simultaneously. The two views are mutually exclusive. There is no way to reconcile the differences between the doctrines of unlimited substitutability and unlimited growth, on the one hand, and Georgescu-Roegen's entropic interpretation of the economic process on the other. It's clear, at the moment, which side most economists have chosen. In spite of the dismal performance of the world economy since the early 1970s, they cling to the faith that technological progress and economic growth will "solve" mankind's problems.

One of the illusions of economics—one probably shared, with appropriate adjustments, by the members of other scholarly bodies— is that research in this field is on the "cutting edge" of new knowledge. In the hard sciences—physics, chemistry, biology—there is abundant evidence that this is, in fact, the case. In the social sciences, however, it isn't necessarily true. This is particularly the case in economics, where the gap between the "promises" of professionals and the performance of the economy is widening. When this gap is perceived by non-economists and they begin to ask embarrassing questions, conventional economics may be in danger. A crack in the edifice might have been started by a book by Jeremy Rifkin (with Ted Howard) entitled *Entropy: A New World View* (The Viking Press, 1980). Rifkin's book is a lucid, non-technical discussion of some of the basic principles of bioeconomics.

"Each day we awake to a world that appears more confused and disordered than the one we left the night before," Rifkin says. "Nothing seems to work anymore. Our leaders are forever lamenting and apologizing." Their attempts to deal with such problems as inflation, unemployment, and shortages "create even greater problems than the one they were meant to solve." We respond by blaming politicians. They respond by blaming one another. It's no surprise that the public is confused. The accounts of economic problems they read or hear are filtered through writers and commentators as uncomprehending of their causes as are the politicians.

Rifkin's book was written for the general public. It includes an "Afterword" by Georgescu-Roegen, which gives it a stamp of legitimacy. If it has the impact which it deserves, this book could force political leaders to consider the ideas which Georgescu-Roegen has been disseminating—in print and in numerous public addresses—for more than a decade. As public awareness of the principles of bioeconomics grows, it will be increasingly difficult for conventional economists to ignore them. The economics profession could be on the brink of the first genuine revolution in economic thought since Adam Smith's *Wealth of Nations*.

Entropy was widely reviewed. The reviews were, on the whole, favorable, even those by reviewers who appeared to be shaken by its message and unwilling to go all the way with its author. One of the first to appear was in *Business Week* (September 8, 1980). It was by Michael Sheldrick, the magazine's energy editor. His review is an apposite example of Keynes's dictum about the tenacity of ideas. Sheldrick's description of the entropic process is excellent; he shows how widely the entropy law applies, and praises Rifkin for the clarity of his exposition.

At no point does he attempt to refute the entropy law. He says, in fact, it is "a fundamental law of physics." But he is unwilling to bite the bullet and follow the law to its logical conclusion. Rifkin's "grim scenario," he says, "leads the author to a solution that, while it may be correct in the abstract, is nonsensical in practice."

Why is it nonsensical? Because "most economists view the economic process as activity that adds order and value to otherwise disorganized and valueless materials. . . ." Isn't it possible, however, that "most economists" could be wrong? Before the Keynesian revolution, most economists believed that free enterprise economies were "self-equilibrating." The ideal economic system, according to the accepted doctrine of that time, was one in which there would be full employment without inflation. Anything that caused either unemployment or inflation was an "interference," and all such interferences, according to the conventional view, should be extirpated.

But Keynes pointed out in 1935 that the British economy had experienced chronic unemployment for almost fifteen years, and the American economy was then in the sixth year of its worst depression. The notion of self-equilibrating tendencies made sense at a time when economic growth was buoyed by territorial expansion. But those tendencies don't work in mature economies. If mature economies are to grow, Keynes insisted, governments will have to intervene to stimulate investment and to maintain consumption at "full employment" levels.

World War II proved Keynes to be right, and most economists jumped on the Keynesian bandwagon during the post-war era. Political leaders also recognized that if wars could produce full employment, government spending on roads, schools, hospitals, and other useful forms of social capital could do the same. The Keynesian revolution had won a sweeping victory.

The idea that stands in the way of adaptation to a new set of global economic conditions today, however, is the Keynesian conclusion that economic growth is not only desirable but necessary. Keynesian economics is demand economics, pure and simple. Keynes didn't discuss supply. Mankind could achieve a Utopian existence, Keynes firmly believed, by maintaining effective demand at full-employment levels. This idea has become as firmly engrained in the thinking of today's conventional economists as the earlier notion about self-equilibrating economic systems which Keynes succeeded in dislodging.

Today's problems are not demand problems, nor are they simply economic problems. The supply problems, which dominate today—whether economists like it or not—are biological and physical as well as economic in nature.

Sheldrick says that "mankind has never willingly given up the fruits of technological progress." He's right. But the key word is "willingly." There was no need to give up the fruits of progress—technological or otherwise—in the past. But one side-effect of technological progress was an increase in the demand for energy. When energy consumption is expressed in a single unit—billions of metric tons of coal, for example—then plotted on a graph which also shows world population growth, the energy-consumption curve lies below the population growth curve until some time in the late 1950s. Since then, however, the energy consumption curve has grown more rapidly than the population curve. This, in its most elemental form, is a description of "the energy problem." The entropy law is older than the planet, but the narrower energy problem is of fairly recent origin.

Sheldrick's statement that Rifkin's "solution" to the entropy problem may be "correct in the abstract but nonsensical in practice" cannot be defended on logical grounds. Either Rifkin's statement is correct, both in the abstract and in practice, or it is wrong in both cases. This is a classical example of the meaningless statement that something is "correct in theory but wrong in practice." If it's wrong in practice the theory is unsound, and no one has suggested that the second law of thermodynamics is an unsound theory.

Bridging the Hard and Soft Sciences

It is not an uncommon view that a major distinction between the physical and social sciences is that the former are characterized by precision of measurement and accuracy of prediction, while the latter are considered to be mushy and to have limited, if any, predictive capability. Evidence to support this position isn't hard to find, but it has nothing to do with the comparative abilities or intellects of physical and social scientists. Physical scientists deal with inanimate matter, mindless life, or the generally predictable behavior of animals. Social scientists deal with the most unpredictable of all creatures— human beings. It's impossible to control the minds and behavior of everyone even in the most ruthless totalitarian society. It's almost hopeless to try to predict the behavior of individuals, with a high degree of accuracy, in a democratic system.

Social scientists, particularly economists, have tried to compensate for the intractability of the "material" they work with by trying to ape the physical sciences. But as Georgescu-Roegen has pointed out, the effort to build a "science" of economics on the laws of

Newtonian physics is what got conventional economics on the wrong track more than a century ago. Recent work by a major physical scientist suggests, however, that the entropy law, in the words of Wil Lepkowski, "could create that long-sought bridge between the physical and social sciences" (*Chemical and Engineering News*, April 16, 1979). The effort mentioned by Lepkowski won the Nobel Prize in Chemistry for Ilya Prigogine in 1977. A non-technical description of this work was provided by Itamar Procaccia and John Ross, of the MIT Department of Chemistry, in the November 18, 1977, issue of *Science*:

> In thermodynamics the second law appears as the evolution law of continuous disorganization, or the disappearance of structure. . . . In biology or in sociology, the idea of evolution is, on the contrary, related to the increase of organization resulting in structure whose complexity is ever increased. Thus the classical thermodynamic point of view indicated that chaos is progressively taking over, whereas biology points in the opposite direction. Are there two different sets of physical laws that need to be involved to account for such differences in behavior? The general conclusion of Prigogine's work is that there is only one type of physical law, but different thermodynamic situations: near and far from equilibrium.

This brilliant idea—which seems intuitively clear, after it has been expressed by someone else—has attracted relativly little attention outside a fairly restricted scientific circle. But it could be one of the more important discoveries of recent times. It strongly reinforces the principles underlying bioeconomics. And it provides a powerful scientific argument in support of the policy prescriptions that follow naturally from an acceptance of those principles.

When a piece of coal has been transformed from a unit of available energy to an equal amount of unavailable energy, in the process of being burned to perform "work," thermodynamic equilibrium has been reached. But as a society progresses from one in which a few dominate the many by the arbitrary and capricious exercise of power—including control over life and death—to one governed by the rule of law, and a more equitable distribution of income and wealth, it becomes more orderly and stable. As this progression occurs, the society moves away from thermodynamic equilibrium. This is the essence of the "Prigogine Bridge" between the physical and the social sciences.

Translated into the ideas developed in the concluding section of the last chapter, Prigogine's discovery indicates that a rational society is able to control the rate at which it approaches thermodynamic equilibrium. We can continue on the path of economic anarchy, which will ultimately lead to the disappearance of structure—to chaos—or we can learn to live cooperatively. But the essence of cooperation, as Raskin noted in his discussion of recent trends in collective bargaining, is a willingness on the part of all concerned to give as well as take.

Cooperation will mean adopting a system of democratic planning along the lines suggested by Leontief. The precise form of that cooperation need not be completely mapped in advance. Adoption of indicative planning would mean giving up some ideas long regarded as immutable truths, and that—as Keynes pointed out—is the hardest part of trying anything new. But the idea of substituting cooperation for confrontation does not mean the abandonment of market economics. It means putting together the most complete, most up-to-date body of economic data we're capable of producing, and using those data to establish constraints, by consensus, within which markets can operate. The only revolution Leontief has called for is an *information* revolution. In the United States it's one that is long past due.

To repeat a point made in the last chapter: if we could count on a revival of robust economic growth, there would be no need for fundamental changes in economic behavior or organization. But the whole point of bioeconomics is that we can no more count on economic growth to "solve" societal problems than a forty-five-year-old adult can count on growth to restore youthful vigor. Under conditions of sustained, robust growth, a lot of economic problems take care of themselves. When a mature economy approaches the end of growth, however, cooperation and planning for the future are more than a couple of choices among a wide range of options. They become categorical imperatives.

Optimism, Pessimism, or Realism?

A hasty reaction to bioeconomics might view it, quite incorrectly, as "warmed-over Malthusianism." Another mistake lumps bioeconomics with the "limits to growth" hypothesis advanced by Dennis and Donella Meadows. In a limited sense—but only in a limited sense—there is an affinity between bioeconomics and their ideas, but they aren't the same.

Malthus, who predicted that population would outrun the means of subsistence, overlooked the potential effects of technological progress; an understandable omission on his part since the idea of progress was formulated only after the industrial revolution was well under way. But there is nothing in bioeconomics which suggests limits to technological progress other than those imposed by the entropy law. Bioeconomics also doesn't include such exercises in long-term forecasting as those engaged in by the Meadows. If everyone had to choose up sides, and go with either the hearty optimism of conventional economics or the pessimism of Malthus-Meadows, bioeconomists would have to incline toward the latter. In fact, however, there is a third option—*realism*.

Georgescu-Roegen doesn't suggest that mankind has to choose between unlimited substitutability and unlimited growth, on the one hand, or imminent catastrophe on the other. Once one accepts the view that the economic process is entropic, however, it follows that if policy makers continue to pursue the goal of unlimited growth the end result will be catastrophe. So what should society do? The policy prescriptions of bioeconomics are the essence of simplicity. They can be expressed in two words: conservation and sharing.

Even conventional economists have little difficulty with the notion of conservation. Indeed, the conventional view has it that there are two possible kinds of conservation: one imposed by fiat (i.e., price controls and rationing) or one imposed by the price system. Most conventional economists would vote for the latter. As various forms of energy and resources become increasingly scarce, they argue, their *relative* prices will rise. That, in turn, will force society to conserve. The trouble with this prescription is its implicit assumption that everyone has an equal chance to bid for scarce resources. We know that isn't true.

Conventional economists have proposed a variety of schemes ranging from negative income taxes to allocations in kind—such as food stamps, fuel stamps, and so forth—to insure that the poor are not entirely frozen out of markets by rising prices. But the price system must be maintained, they insist, to provide incentives. Incentives for what? For invention, innovation, discovery—anything that will stimulate economic growth.

More and faster growth is the only acceptable answer to contemporary economic problems within the limited vision of the conventional economist. But how long could this go on? As the physicist Albert Bartlett has demonstrated again and again, growth cannot go on indefinitely in a finite world, and the world we live in is finite. Those who dream of exploiting the resources of other planets, of space colonization, or similar "solutions" live in a world of fantasy.

If one had to choose between the probability that mankind and progress either will be "saved" by some massive technological breakthrough or will be visited by global catastrophe—given our present knowledge, and reasonable possibilities for the remainder of this century—the odds would lie heavily on the side of catastrophe. The probability that either the price system or a major technological breakthrough will "get the world economy moving again" is extremely low. But robust growth *or* catastrophe are not the only choices open to mankind. A third possibility is learning to live cooperatively with little or no growth.

Economics and Ethics

One major distinction between conventional economics and bioeconomics has yet to be made. This one is likely to cause more difficulty for most economists than Georgescu-Roegen's distinction between mechanistic and entropic processes. Bioeconomics includes ethical considerations as well as economic, biological, and thermodynamic principles. This was implied earlier when sharing was paired with conservation. Actually, the idea of conservation can be subsumed under the notion of sharing because it means, essentially, that each generation must share the world's limited dowry of energy and resources with future generations. But how is this to be done? Georgescu-Roegen provides few specific guidelines on this score. The details of programs to insure conservation and redistribution have not concerned him as much as the principles. He feels, evidently, that education and volunteerism—as well as enlightened leadership—will reduce waste and the more extreme forms of conspicuous consumption. Redistribution could be carried out, at a moderate pace, under present fiscal arrangements. Various policy options could be explored. But they won't be—as long as the illusion remains that the problems of unemployment, inflation, and the present maldistribution of wealth can be solved or mitigated by the revival of economic growth.

Bioeconomics and Technology

The standard answer to contemporary economic problems is the *deus ex machina* of the "technological fix." Does the entropic nature of the economic process preclude the possibility of major technological developments? Not at all. Technology, after all, deals with ideas, not with hardware. The world will need all the useful new ideas it can develop, for as far ahead as we can see, if conditions aren't to get substantially worse as a growing population presses inexorably on a diminishing stock of non-renewable resources. The one notion of a technical fix which is incompatible with bioeconomics is that at some time in the future there will be a great breakthrough which will reverse the entropic process. That is as likely as the discovery of a process which would repeal the law of gravity, or one which would permit human life to be extended indefinitely. Those who believe such things are possible can't possibly be reached by the message of bioeconomics.

A Bioeconomic World: What Would It Be Like?

What would life be like in a society in which the principles of bioeconomics were widely accepted? No one really knows. It would be easy, as Herman Kahn has done, to make quantitative forecasts—with very wide upper and lower limits—of economic conditions 200 years from now. After all, no one presently living will be around to check on their accuracy; so it's a pointless, if not a fatuous, exercise. The only thing we know with certainty is that in 200 years life on this planet will be vastly different.

It is possible to consider broad alternatives and general guidelines. Basically, mankind can adjust in an orderly manner to a world of growing scarcities, declining productivity, and lower real incomes. Or there can be a strong drift toward a new *laissez faire* and the nihilism that would engender.

In terms of the Prigogine Bridge, we have a choice. Society can continue the long-term trend toward increasing order, and greater cooperation, by moving away from thermodynamic equilibrium. Or it can drift *toward* that equilibrium and certain chaos.

Not much more can be said if society chooses nihilism. Eventually we'll cannibalize each other in a Darwinian struggle of the survival of the richest. But if society chooses the path toward order rather than chaos, some broad if necessarily imprecise guidelines seem clear.

There will be a revival of *thrift* as a guiding principle. Society will make a concerted effort to cut out waste in all its forms. Thrift shouldn't be confused with *austerity*. Instead of seeing how little we can get by with, which is what austerity means, we'll see how much we can get out of what is available.

Thrift, of course, leads to conservation. But again there can be a "minimax" rule. Get as much work as possible (max) out of as little energy as we can get by with (min).

The probability is high that there will be a long-run trend toward more labor-intensive, energy-saving production processes where these are feasible. That would not only conserve energy and resources, it would also help solve the unemployment problem. No one suggests a return to the "cottage system." Future industrial complexes will consist of a mix of large- and small-scale establishments. But in a society in which energy conservation becomes a major policy objective, relatively small, labor-intensive establishments are likely to grow at the expense of large, capital—(and energy)—intensive ones.

Present disparities in income and wealth will not survive in a no-growth society. There will have to be redistribution—among income classes, among regions, and among nations. This imperative does not assume a great increase in altruism. Redistribution will be motivated more by fear than goodness of heart. If the poor aren't given an opportunity to earn more in the future than they have in the past, there will be a greater propensity for them to take what they can get.

Redistribution won't mean equality. It will mean a *tendency* toward greater equality. No one can predict how far it will go. A few trends are highly predictable, however. The United States, with 6 percent of the world's population, will not be able to continue consuming 30 percent of the world's annual production of basic energy (coal, oil, and natural gas) and approximately the same annual proportion of the world's output of goods and services. This share has, in fact, started to drop, however slowly, and that trend is certain to be accelerated. We need have no illusions about enjoying all this, but we also should have no illusions about the alternatives. We will go along with a trend toward greater equality in the global distribution of income and wealth out of ethical considerations or because we want to avoid the consequences of *failing to share* what we have with others whose deprivation is increasing rather than diminishing. We know the world has become highly interdependent. It will become even more interdependent in the future.

World population will grow from the present 4 or 4.5 billion to something in excess of 6 billion souls by the turn of the century, and there's no reason to believe it will stop suddenly in the year 2000. When we realize that about 80 percent of the present population lives at or close to a subsistence level, only mindless optimists can believe that the world economy will continue to function in the future as it has in the past. In a sparsely populated world there was always the escape valve of unoccupied space. For practical purposes this option no longer exists. We can fight it out—although we already know about "no-win wars"—or we can learn to live together in a modest degree of harmony.

One can only hope that Lewis Thomas is right when he says: "The urge to form partnerships, to link up in collaborative arrangements, is perhaps the oldest, strongest, and most fundamental force in nature."

If he is, and if this urge prevails, mankind can survive for a long time if not necessarily for the millenia Thomas confidently expects. A detailed article, "The Evolution of Cooperation" by Robert Axelrod and William D. Hamilton (*Science*, March 21, 1981), elaborates on the theme which Thomas touched only in passing.

Thomas believes that we have a genetic urge to be useful. But this urge is thwarted when we work in ever-larger groups. "Larger collections of us, cities for instance, hardly ever get anything right. And, of course, there is the modern nation, probably the most stupefying example of biological error since the age of the great reptiles—wrong at every turn."

All nations, of course, are affected by the entropic process. Again, one can only hope that the Prigogine principle will work; that as the world's stocks of energy and resources are steadily transformed from their usable forms into waste, mankind will develop highly structured cooperative organizations. The outcome of the race between the evolution of a cooperative society and destructive nihilism is at best in doubt. As Carroll Pursell put it in his review of Rifkin's *Entropy* (*New York Times Book Review*, October 26, 1980), "We never save time by using energy—rather by using up energy we destroy time itself. It's an old message, but one that becomes increasingly important as time runs out."

SELECTED REFERENCES

Books

Barney, Gerald O., *et al. The Global 2000 Report to the President.* Prepared by the Environmental Protection Agency and the Department of State. Vol. I, *Entering the 21st Century;* Vol. II, *The Technical Report.* Washington, D.C.: U.S. Government Printing Office, 1980.

Bent, Henry A. *The Second Law: An Introduction to Classical and Statistical Thermodynamics.* New York: Oxford University Press, 1965.

Brown, Lester R. *In the Human Interest.* New York: W. W. Norton & Company, 1974.

Denison, Edward F. *Accounting for Slower Economic Growth.* Washington, D.C.: The Brookings Institution, 1979.

Ehrenfeld, David. *The Arrogance of Humanism.* New York: Oxford University Press, 1978.

Georgescu-Roegen, Nicholas. *Demain la Décroissance.* Preface by Ivo Rens and Jacques Grinevald. Paris: Pierre-Marcel Favre, 1979.

_____. *Energy and Economic Myths.* New York: Pergamon Press, Inc., 1976.

_____. *The Entropy Law and the Economic Process.* Cambridge, MA: Harvard University Press, 1973.

Gilder, George. *Wealth and Poverty.* New York: Basic Books, 1981.

Hicks, John R. *The Theory of Wages.* London: Macmillan, 1963.

Joint Committee on the Economic Report. *Economic Growth from 1976-1986: Problems, Prospects, and Patterns.* Washington, D.C.: U.S. Government Printing Office, 1976.

Kahn, Herman, *et al. The Next 200 Years.* New York: William Morrow and Company, Inc., 1976.

Keynes, John Maynard. *The General Theory of Employment, Interest and Money.* New York: Harcourt-Brace, 1935.

Meadows, Donella H., *et al. The Limits to Growth.* New York: Universe Books, 1972.

Miernyk, William H., *et al. Regional Impacts of Rising Energy Prices.* Cambridge, MA: Ballinger, 1978.

Mishan, Ezra J. *The Costs of Economic Growth*. New York: Praeger, 1967.

O'Neill, Gerard K. *The High Frontier*. New York: William Morrow and Company, Inc., 1977.

_____. *2081*. New York: Simon & Schuster, 1981.

Renshaw, Edward F. *The End of Progress: Adjusting to a No-Growth Economy*. North Scituate, MA: Duxbury Press, 1976.

Rifkin, Jeremy. *Entropy*. New York: The Viking Press, 1980.

Schumacher, E. F. *Small Is Beautiful: Economics as if People Mattered*. New York: Harper & Row, 1973.

Simon, Julian L. *The Ultimate Resource*. Princeton, NJ: Princeton University Press, 1981.

Smith, V. Kerry. *Scarcity and Growth Reconsidered*. Baltimore, MD: The Johns Hopkins University Press, 1979.

Stobaugh, Robert, and Daniel Yergin, *et al. Energy Future*. New York: Random House, 1979.

Thomas, Lewis. *The Lives of a Cell*. New York: The Viking Press, 1974.

_____. *The Medusa and the Snail*. New York: The Viking Press, 1979.

Thurow, Lester C. *The Zero-Sum Society*. New York: Basic Books, 1980.

Toffler, Alvin. *The Third Wave*. New York: William Morrow and Company, Inc., 1980.

Zamagni, Stefano. *Georgescu-Roegen, i Fondamenti Della Teoria del Consumatore*. Milan: Estas Libri, 1979.

Articles

Bartlett, Albert A. "Forgotten Fundamentals of the Energy Crisis," *American Journal of Physics*, 46 (September 1978), pp. 876–888.

Georgescu-Roegen, Nicholas. "A Bioeconomic Viewpoint," *Review of Social Economy*, 35:3 (December 1977), pp. 361–375.

_____. "Energy Analysis and Economic Valuation," *The Southern Economic Journal*, 45 (April 1979), pp. 1023–1058.

_____. "Energy and Economic Myths," *The Southern Economic Journal*, 41 (January 1975), pp. 347–381.

_____. "Myths About Energy and Matter," *Growth and Change*, 10 (January 1979), pp. 16–22.

_____. "The Steady-State and Ecological Salvation," *BioScience*, 27 (April 1977), pp. 266–269.

Goeller, H. E., and A. M. Weinberg. "The Age of Substitutability," *The American Economic Review*, 68:6 (December 1978), pp. 1–11.

Gowdy, John M. "Radical Economics and Resource Scarcity," *Review of Social Economy*, 39 (October 1981), pp. 165–180.

Hardin, Garrett. "Dr. Pangloss Meets Cassandra," *The New Republic* (October 28, 1981), pp. 31–34.

Miernyk, William H. "Energy Future, A Review Article," *West Virginia Law Review*, 82:4 (1980), pp. 1257–1275.

Stone, Richard. "Whittling Away at the Residual: Some Thoughts on Denison's Growth Accounting," *Journal of Economic Literature*, 18 (December 1980), pp. 1539–1543.

About the Author

William H. Miernyk is Claude Worthington Bene-
dum Professor of Economics in the College of
Mineral and Energy Resources and Director of the
Regional Research Institute at West Virginia University. He received his B.A. degree from the
University of Colorado and the M.A. and Ph.D.
degrees from Harvard University.

He formerly taught at Northeastern University
and the University of Colorado, and was Visiting
Professor of Economics at the Massachusetts Institute of Technology in 1957-58 and at Harvard
University in 1969-70. He served as a consultant to
the U.S. Senate Committee on Commerce and the
Special Committee on Unemployment Problems; to
the Appalachian Regional Commission; and on advisory committees in the U.S. Departments of
Commerce and Labor. He also has been a consultant to A. D. Little, Inc., the Batelle Institute, the
Brookings Institution, and CONSAD.